FORENSIC CARDIOVASCULAR MEDICINE

FORENSIC CARDIOVASCULAR MEDICINE

BASIL RUDUSKY, MD
FACA, FASA, FACP, FCCP, FACC, FAGS, FACFE

CRC Press
Taylor & Francis Group
Boca Raton London New York

CRC Press is an imprint of the
Taylor & Francis Group, an **informa** business

CRC Press
Taylor & Francis Group
6000 Broken Sound Parkway NW, Suite 300
Boca Raton, FL 33487-2742

Printed in the United States of America on acid-free paper
10 9 8 7 6 5 4 3 2 1

International Standard Book Number-13: 978-1-4200-9431-2 (Hardcover)

Library of Congress Cataloging-in-Publication Data

RuDusky, Basil M.
Forensic cardiovascular medicine / Basil M. RuDusky.
p. cm.
Includes bibliographical references and index.
ISBN 978-1-4200-9431-2 (alk. paper)
1. Forensic cardiology. I. Title.

RA1170.H4R83 2009
614'.1--dc22 2008045228

Visit the Taylor & Francis Web site at
http://www.taylorandfrancis.com

and the CRC Press Web site at
http://www.crcpress.com

Section III
VASCULAR ABNORMALITIES

Section IV
SPECIFIC CARDIOPATHIC DISORDERS

Section V
TOXIC AND PHYSICAL INFLUENCES

Contents

Dedication

To those in the medical and legal professions who possess the highest qualities of honesty, integrity, and independence in formulating their opinions and conclusions.

Preface

In formulating the concept for the development of this book, it was my intent to draw upon a portion of my vast experience to emphasize some of the most frequently encountered cardiovascular medical problems facing the physician in his or her position as an independent medical examiner or forensic medical specialist. To cover the field in its entirety, an entire textbook of medicine would need to be rewritten, which goes far beyond the scope and purpose of this text. I believe the initial goals have been accomplished, so that future editions can expand in overall content and continue to update the important basic foundations applied to the first edition. I hope this book will justifiably serve as the keystone in assisting the medical and legal professions, as well as the judiciary, in their complicated and overburdened task of applying scientific information, medical knowledge, and reasoning in making their conclusions and difficult decisions regarding standards of care and medical/legal causation.

Emphasis is placed on those conditions and disease states that are apt to be overlooked, misdiagnosed, or tardily considered—those that often require a certain degree of clinical acumen and perspicacity. It is in these situations that the frequency of medical, legal, and judicial interventions becomes enhanced. This is especially important in the diagnosis of the six conditions that the author emphasizes the attending and consulting physicians must be constantly aware of and cannot afford to overlook.

Basil M. RuDusky, MD

Acknowledgments

The author expresses his deepest appreciation and gratitude to Denise Maxfield Marycz for her indefatigable computerization of the entire text. Her remarkable ability to read and interpret my handwriting made our difficult task much less burdensome.

The assistance of Thomas Gurzinski of the Wyoming Valley Health Care System in the preparation of figures and tables was of immense value to Denise and myself.

I extend my thanks to Becky Masterman and David Fausel of the Taylor and Francis Group for their editorial supervision of all matters pertaining to the publication of this book.

In closing, it is appropriate to recognize the support of my wife Bernadine, whose assistance and logistical endeavors were, as always, greatly appreciated.

Basil M. RuDusky, MD

About the Author

Dr. Basil M. RuDusky, MD, has been in the private practice of cardiology, internal medicine and forensic medicine for over 40 years. He is the author of numerous scientific articles and papers, three books, two short stories and one poem.

Dr. RuDusky has served in numerous consulting positions for the federal government, large corporations, insurance companies, and independent medical service agencies. He also serves on the manuscript review board for several medical journals and is associate editor of *Angiology*, the official international journal of the American Society of Angiology and the International Academy of Clinical and Applied Thrombosis/Hemostasis.

Dr. RuDusky's medical and science-associated memberships and fellowships are as extensive as his accolades and commendations, lending stature to his international reputation in clinical and forensic cardiovascular medicine. He is a diplomat of the American Board of Internal Medicine and the American Board of Forensic Medicine and is a fellow of the American College of Angiology, the American Society of Angiology, the American College of Physicians, the American College of Cardiology, the College of Chest Physicians, the American College of Forensic Examiners, and the American Geriatric Society.

Overview of Forensic Medicine

I

1 Introduction and Philosophy

The changing social and scientific structure of our society is, in part, responsible for the growth and development of forensic medicine and forensic pathology. A reasonable definition of forensic medicine, in contrast to that of forensic pathology, is necessary and justified. Forensic pathology is generally applied to conclusions formulated as to the basis of the end result of a criminal act, whether or not death has been the endpoint. Forensic medicine is adequately defined as the application of the principles and practice of all fields of medicine to matters that have become involved in judicial proceedings, criminal and civil. The forensic medical specialist may be limited to his or her particular specialty or field of interest, or must have an extensive knowledge of medicine in general. This includes not only all aspects and subspecialties of internal medicine, but also the associated medical and surgical specialties for which the internist is called upon for medical consultation and subsequent care. The background of the forensic medical specialist generally originates from one's practice as an independent medical examiner in a particular field of specialized medicine or general internal medicine. This would also include all surgical specialties, psychiatry, and nursing. The tasks appointed to the independent medical examiner and the forensic medical specialist are often similar, thus frequently producing a unification of these two very important facets of medical–legal medicine.

It cannot be emphasized too strongly that regardless of a physician's primary interest or specialty, he or she must possess a vast amount of medical knowledge complemented by the advantage of considerable experience. This includes the ability to quickly and accurately recall brief conclusions from the endless medical literature on pertinent subjects.

It is the duty of medical examiners to perform their tasks in accordance with the following principles.

1. Quantitative assessment
2. Qualitative evaluation
3. Accuracy
4. Honesty
5. Independent neutrality

These tasks are often very difficult to fully and adequately perform without considerable experience. Lack of experience is often the major flaw in the system, and when accompanied by a lack of knowledge, it creates a disastrous situation. When accompanied by dishonesty, the situation becomes disgustingly tragic. Physicians so engaged are frequently of limited knowledge, and even more frequently have less experience than is required to enable them to complete an intelligent review and assessment of a specific case. This results in their coming to a conclusion that is very often unsatisfactory and erroneous. The legal and judicial reviews and opinions derived from such a conclusion are thus made more difficult and are often flawed because of inaccurate or inadequate medical evaluation and testimony.

The independent medical examiner must possess the current editions of the major textbooks of internal medicine, as well as an appropriate representation of other fields of medicine, surgery, and their allied subspecialties—a necessary and desirable task not often accomplished by most physicians. A reasonably rapid reference source to the medical literature is a necessity. Often, it is the research one does on a particular problem or case that determines its eventual outcome.

Experienced physicians realize that opinions derived from death certificates are notoriously inaccurate as to not only the principal cause of death, but also the associated sequential conditions leading to the cause of death. These data are often found to be illogical in their pathologic physiology or sequence.

Even more lacking on the part of many physicians is their knowledge of what constitutes disability regarding the many disease states and abnormal conditions that they evaluate or treat. This makes everyone's job more difficult—the lawyers, compensation referees, judges, independent medical examiners, and claims adjusters. This can be a costly matter to both the plaintiff and the defendant. It must be constantly remembered that all of the above nonmedical professionals must make responsible and critical judgments based upon medical reports and testimony. These reports must be relied upon by the legal, judicial, and insurance structures to arrive at a responsible and just decision. There is no place for the physician who lies or bends the facts to favor his patient or client. The entire social and economic structure is done great harm by these types of actions. A physician must be willing to lose a patient under these circumstances rather than prostitute himself by falsely favoring a patient or client. The practice of medicine in any of its facets cannot be subjugated to any form of dishonesty. Many retailers and manufacturers have come to the realization that "honesty is the best policy." Unfortunately, the practice of medicine has not yet fulfilled that necessary and admirable goal under any and all circumstances.

Death Certificates, Autopsies, and Medical Experts

2

Death certificates are an important part of medical statistics and epidemiologic studies. They serve an important role in this regard but are notoriously inaccurate.

A study of the Framingham data in 1998 for coding coronary heart disease as the cause of death revealed a 7.9–24.3% overestimated frequency of coronary heart disease and as much as a twofold increase in older persons.[1]

A study of 494 death certificates and their comparison to autopsy reports revealed that only 59% were properly completed, and 49% contained disagreements.[2]

Another study reported a correctly reported cause of death in 56.9% of cases by internists, 56.0% by residents, and 55.7% by students, indicating an equal level of error by these three groups.[3]

A report on completing death certificates by residents indicated a low 23% optimal scoring range, with 45% incorrectly identifying a cardiovascular event as the primary cause of death.[4]

More recently, an evaluation of death certificates involving sudden cardiac death found an overestimation by physicians of 47%, suggesting that out-of-hospital coronary heart disease death rates derived from death certificates should be interpreted with caution.[5]

Autopsy studies have consistently documented a substantial discrepancy between clinical and autopsy diagnoses over several decades. A recent study reported an overall median major error rate of 23.5% and a class I median error rate of 9.0%. It concluded that although the autopsy illumination of unsuspected diagnoses has decreased over time, ongoing use of the autopsy is warranted.[6]

Kassirer and Cecil, in a philosophic review of the inconsistency of evidentiary statements for medical testimony, concluded, "The medical and legal professions have a tradition of worriness that has impeded effective cooperation in developing consistent standards from the medical profession to assist them in strengthening the role of medical testimony…, (they) should respond by correcting misrepresentations… and assist in the development of standards…."[7]

Although most expert witnesses are capable and qualified, the so-called "hired-gun" or "pay-for-hire to say anything experts" are wreaking havoc on the medical–legal system. Injudicious and highly prejudicial testimony is running rampant in the system and creating an economic hardship, which has gone beyond the normally expected proportion of justifiable lawsuits in our present litigious society.

Financial greed is the basis of frivolous or unjustified lawsuits and is out of control to the point where malpractice premiums have escalated to a level of near destruction of the medical profession. Unless state and federal regulation of appropriate and substantial impact are forthcoming, a national economic and health burden will reach a critical point and seriously affect our health delivery system. In 35 years of serving as a totally independent expert for defense and plaintiff malpractice claims, the author has never seen a "bad" doctor get sued. It has only been the better and conscientious ones that have suffered the burden.

II
Cardiac Trauma

3 Myocardial Contusion and Blunt Cardiac Trauma

Overview

Blunt chest trauma producing blunt cardiac trauma is becoming increasingly prevalent. Its occurrence has been increasing over the past three decades. The more obvious contributing factors involved in the increased incidence have been motor vehicle accidents, sports injuries, accidental injuries of all sorts, and criminally-induced trauma.

The most common cause of blunt cardiac trauma is the motor vehicle accident. It is a matter of debate as to the implied decrease due to seat belts, and of lesser debate since the advent of the airbag. Cardiac injury can occur because of direct trauma to the chest wall, as well as by forces involved in deceleration during such accidents. Injury to the heart can also be produced by crushing abdominal and pelvic trauma of severe magnitude.

The commonest injury to the heart produced by blunt chest trauma is myocardial contusion. Statistically, the motor vehicle accident remains the number-one culprit. Sports injuries to the chest caused by a baseball, hockey puck, and karate kick are known to produce cardiac trauma. Although seat belts have decreased the incidence of chest and cardiac trauma caused by hitting the steering wheel, they have not eliminated those caused by the deceleration forces associated with high-speed motor vehicle accidents. As previously noted, it has been generally accepted that air-bags will decrease the incidence of injuries to the chest and heart, but no statistics are presently available.

Cardiac injury secondary to blunt chest trauma has a probable incidence of 15 to 17%, with myocardial contusion being predominant.[8] Autopsy studies of patients who died as a result of severe body trauma due to automobile accidents revealed the incidence of cardiac trauma to be as high as 76%.

Significant injuries to organs in the chest can occur from nonpenetrating blunt trauma even in the absence of external evidence of injury to the chest wall and in the absence of rib or sternal fractures. The latter is especially true in children and young adults because of greater elasticity (pliability) of the structural chest anatomy. The proximal aorta may be torn from its myocardial root following a motor vehicle collision, causing sudden death with no evidence of external chest trauma.

Mechanism of Blunt Cardiac Injury

Compression of the heart between the sternum and vertebrae can produce direct trauma to the heart. Trauma can also be produced by sudden, forceful acceleration or deceleration as the heart swings like a pendulum and hits the anterior chest wall or vertebrae. The forceful stretching and twisting of the heart due to its suspension and attachments in the chest may also produce injury.

Abdominal crush injuries, if severe, can transmit sufficient hydrostatic force to the heart by way of the great vessels. The resultant increase in intracardiac chamber pressure can be severe enough to cause an internal contusion or can rupture a valve leaflet or the myocardium. This type of injury is more likely to occur during the phase of the cardiac cycle when the heart is filled with blood, the isovolumic and isometric phases of mechanical and electrical activity and myocardial function. Therefore, the consequences of traumatic injury to the heart can be a matter of fate, as well as the physical factors involved. Injuries may be more or less extensive, depending on when the instantaneous trauma occurs during the cardiac cycle (systole or diastole) as well as during which phase of electrical activity is present during the contraction–relaxation cycles of the ventricles. The heart is more detrimentally affected by the impending blow during the isometric phase.

As previously stated and worth reiterating, the most common nonpenetrating traumatic cardiac injury is an uncomplicated myocardial contusion. The terminology is simple, as myocardial contusion implies that the heart muscle has been "bruised." Myocardial contusion has an exceptionally broad scope of magnitude. The injury may be one that is negligible or nondiagnostic and of no significance, or it can be one that is seriously morbid with a multitude of medical complications. It can also have a fatal outcome as a result of the various subsequent complications arising from the injury to the structures of the heart or to the myocardium in general. (See the appendix for the first complete classification of myocardial contusion).

Pathology of Contusion

Depending upon the magnitude of the injury, pathologic evaluation in the mildest cases reveals that the myocardial cells in the vicinity of the contusion generally maintain their structural integrity. In these cases, there is little or no necrosis of the myocardial cells, and healing occurs without fibrosis or scarring. A contusion implies a bruise, a certain degree of extravasation of blood into tissue. Microscopically, this is seen as a collection of blood cells and can be accompanied by myofibrillar degeneration. The healing in such circumstances occurs very quickly, from days to a few weeks, depending on the extent and magnitude of the injury in terms of quantitative and qualitative analysis. In moderately severe cases, areas of fibrosis occur upon healing and are caused by disruption of myocytes and excessive hemorrhage. Varying degrees and areas of myocardial fibrosis may be the end result of moderate cardiac contusion, and these are usually clinically insignificant. The end stage of severe trauma to the myocardium results in myocardial necrosis and scar formation and may cause aneurysmal development in any cardiac chamber. Aneurysm formation may lead to subsequent rupture, with or without pseudoaneurysm formation, and usually culminates in sudden death.

Depending on whether a chest injury is primarily a deceleration injury or a crushing injury, either one or both ventricles or septa may be involved either anteriorly or posteriorly, the results usually being catastrophic. Minute focal lacerations accompanied by interstitial hemorrhage may occur and can be precipitated by blunt injury to the heart when the ventricles are filled with blood.

Larger and more severe areas of injury to the heart muscle usually produce medical consequences and, if survival occurs, heal with resultant scars similar to those seen in cases of acute myocardial infarction, even though a coronary artery was not injured.

Forensic Consideration

Litigation concerning claims of posttraumatic cardiac injury has been steadily increasing. This increase has often been due to a presumption of injury or cardiac problem actually unrelated to an injury or, in fact, without substantial evidence for aggravation of the claimants' prior cardiac status.

It is especially important in cases of suspected or proven myocardial contusion that the forensic medical specialist obtains as much previous medical history, information, and records regarding the presence of previous heart problems as possible.

A history of coronary heart disease, hypertension, diabetes, cardiomegaly, heart murmurs, interventional procedures, heart failure, angina pectoris, myocardial infarction, and so on, is a prerequisite to making a final diagnosis and conclusion.

Electrocardiograms prior to the injury can be invaluable in final decision-making and for medical–legal deposition. The information obtained will serve (usually at some later time) in the proper handling and management of claims based on criminal prosecution, civil suits, malpractice claims, insurance claims, disability and workers' compensation.

Information conscientiously obtained and properly evaluated by an expert can be the determining factor in making or breaking a case that is presented for legal evaluation and subsequent judicial decision. As in all situations, the forensic medical specialist must be thoroughly knowledgeable, highly experienced, and as neutral and independent as possible. This is the basis upon which every case should be accepted and evaluated, for only then can honesty and justice be properly served.

The medical–legal implications of blunt chest trauma are horrendous in terms of cost and time, and all too often are plagued by erroneous or fallacious argumentation and reasoning. Careful clinical observation and skillful diagnostic ability combined with knowledge and experience are mandatory to attempt to resolve the complicated issues involved. A properly and carefully performed postmortem examination is helpful, but even under these circumstances the final decision can be difficult and insecure. One must take into account the type of injury, its location and extent, especially in relationship to the heart structures involved, and the possibility of myocardial pathology resulting from nontraumatic pathophysiology. Especially important are the implications of neurogenic stimulation and the resultant catecholamine release and shock as important factors in producing coronary vasospasm, plaque rupture, and cardiac dysrhythmia.

It cannot be overemphasized that whenever possible, one should obtain all of the available information regarding the historical presence of heart problems prior to the injury. These data should include electrocardiograms, chest x-rays, echocardiograms, ambulatory ECG reports, stress tests, heart scans, cardiac catheterization reports, hospital records, office records, and consultation records. Historical data relating to heart murmurs, cardiomegaly, symptoms of coronary insufficiency, cardiovascular drug therapy, and invasive or surgical intervention are especially important and, if present, are an obligatory requirement.

Frivolous and fallacious lawsuits claiming various inconsequential results of presumed or actual blunt chest trauma are becoming increasingly prevalent in our present highly litigious society. Some, based on inept or inadequate knowledge, are honestly undertaken, whereas others are based upon "expert witness" review and testimony that is bereft of knowledge and experience or is simply fraudulent. Most unfortunately, lawsuits of this type have resulted in unjustified financial gain on the one hand and considerable financial loss on the other. These disgraceful and unfounded results are due simply to the fact that not all lawyers, patients, physicians, and other types of expert witnesses are honest, and, in fact, are lacking in self-respect and integrity.

Symptoms

The symptoms that result from blunt cardiac trauma can range from none to very severe (Table 3.1).

Symptoms generally depend upon the degree of trauma produced, its extent and the anatomic location of the injury, and the immediate and subsequent pathology produced. It is important, and sometimes very difficult, for

Table 3.1 Symptoms That may be Associated with Blunt Chest Trauma and Myocardial Contusion

Chest wall pain
Musculoskeletal pain
Neuromuscular pain
Pseudo-angina
Angina pectoris
Pericardial pain
Pleural pain
Arterial dissection pain
Dyspnea
Lightheadedness
Presyncope
Syncope
Dizziness
Palpitations
Rapid heart beat

the attending physician to separate chest wall symptomatology from symptoms of cardiac origin. The commonest symptom produced is usually chest pain. It is often difficult to differentiate musculoskeletal chest pain from cardiac pain. It is also important to realize the possibility of other causes of chest pain, for example, pain arising from lung injury, which produces pleural pain, or the severe "tearing" type pain of aortic dissection.

Cardiac pain occasionally may be anginal, but is generally pseudo-anginal and is not relieved by nitroglycerin. It can result from a badly contused myocardium or from pericardial inflammation, with or without hemopericardium or pericardial effusion. If the pain is characteristically anginal, especially if intermittent, and is relieved by nitroglycerin, then coronary arterial injury should be suspected. If the patient has a known history of coronary artery disease, the anginal symptoms need not be due to coronary arterial injury but may be associated with vasospasm secondary to the anxiety state shortly following the accident. Unstable angina can occur and may be associated with plaque rupture, depending, of course, on the original pathology. Persistent cardiac pain may be the result of myocardial necrosis, with or without coronary arterial injury or occlusion.

Weakness, dyspnea, presyncope, and syncope are signs of serious injury and may be due to heart or vascular injury or that of other organ systems.

One should carefully look for signs of chest wall bruising, a fractured sternum, or rib fractures, as these can be considered potentially morbid indications of possible cardiac injury. An imprint of the steering wheel or the manufacturer's emblem on the chest, still present in the emergency room shortly after the accident, is an ominous sign in the author's experience.

Preexisting cardiac pathology may make the heart more vulnerable to the various insults produced by blunt chest trauma. This is especially true in cases of suspected coronary arterial injury. This does not imply, however, that postinjury anginal chest pain or myocardial infarction are produced directly by the trauma. Patients with a known history of coronary artery disease may suffer either angina or myocardial infarction as a result of the emotional stress caused by the accident. The consequences of stress affecting the coronary arterial system generally occur within 1 to 2 hours following the precipitating event, and in almost all cases occur in less than 12 to 24 hours. One can therefore easily recognize the previously emphasized necessity and importance of the preexisting condition and medical data, the injury sustained, and the peri-injury and follow-up data. These are invaluable in assisting in final decision-making and in formulating a proper conclusion.

Signs

Signs of cardiac injury may vary as much as the symptoms previously discussed. They range from none to severe or intermittent to relentlessly persistent (Table 3.2)

Tachycardia, predominantly sinus tachycardia, is present in most cases of myocardial contusion and therefore may be stated as being the commonest arrhythmia associated with blunt cardiac trauma. One must be certain to omit other associated causes and comorbid conditions resulting from noncardiac trauma. Foremost is hemorrhage from organ or blood vessel tears and extensive muscle and skeletal injuries. If no other significant noncardiac injuries are found, then one can postulate that the sinus tachycardia is the result of the myocardial contusion, provided that uncontrolled coexisting medical conditions are ruled out, for example, metabolic-electrolyte imbalance, uncontrolled hypertension, coronary arterial occlusive disease with

Table 3.2 Clinical Signs That may be Associated with Blunt Cardiac Trauma

Tachycardia
Hypotension
Cardiac arrhythmia
Congestive heart failure
Pulsus paradoxus
Pulsus alternans
Aggravation of hypertension (pain, sympathetic response)
External signs of chest trauma (bruise, ecchymosis, lacerations, sternal fracture, rib fractures)
Heart murmurs

painless angina (silent ischemia), and emotional disturbance. Hypotension resulting from myocardial contusion alone is an ominous sign and merits immediate extensive investigation and intensive observation, just as it would from any other injury or illness.

Every type of cardiac arrhythmia can be associated with cardiac contusion. Following the usual sinus tachycardia, premature atrial or premature ventricular extrasystoles are the next most common dysrhythmias associated with myocardial contusion. In order of decreasing frequency are atrial tachycardia, atrial fibrillation, and ventricular tachycardia. Bundle branch block and A-V heart block of the first and second degree may also occur. Complete or third-degree A-V block is rare, but always possible. The type of arrhythmia produced is dependent not only on the extent and location of the trauma, but on other associated preinjury and postinjury states such as coronary artery disease, uncontrolled hypertension, cardiomyopathic disease of various etiologies, valvular heart disease, and the presence of cardiac decompensation. The majority of cardiac arrhythmias produced by uncomplicated myocardial contusion are self-limited and chronotropically benign. Even those requiring immediate therapy are usually self-limiting over a short period of time (hours, days, or a few weeks).

Congestive heart failure that is not preexistent is an equally ominous sign and may or may not be associated with hypotension. If other preexistent cardiac pathologies can be excluded, it is a sign of severe, extensive heart muscle damage or accompanying muscle laceration, valvular insufficiency, or myocardial infarction. Large atrial or ventricular septal tears must also be excluded. The presence of pulsus paradoxus or pulsus alternans also should be heeded, as they are important signs of myocardial dysfunction.

Diagnosis

Cardiac contusion has been appropriately called "a diagnostic dilemma."[9] The diagnosis of myocardial contusion is frequently overlooked, especially when uncomplicated, and equally as frequently over-diagnosed when it is, in fact, not present. In its mildest form, it may actually be clinically undetectable and therefore of no actual or practical significance. The increase in more sophisticated diagnostic techniques has made the diagnosis more compatible with that of clinical judgment, but the diagnosis of myocardial contusion still requires the combination of knowledge based on experience and their applicability to good diagnostic acumen. First and foremost in the diagnostic spectrum is suspicion. What is generally not thought of, or considered, is usually not diagnosed—a basic rule of clinical diagnosis.

In the author's experience, it is not unusual to confront attending physicians who diagnose myocardial contusion merely on the basis of blunt chest

Table 3.3 Modalities That can be Utilized in the Diagnosis of Myocardial Contusion

Electrocardiography
Echocardiography
Cardiac enzymes
Cardiac scintography
Chest radiography
Cardiac catheterization

trauma and the presence of chest pain. These situations propagate much legal difficulty and contribute greatly to the unnecessary costs of subsequent medical care. It is also fairly common to see physicians using a single abnormality in the diagnostic armamentarium (Table 3.3) as the basis for diagnosing myocardial contusion.

Electrocardiography and cardiac enzyme determinations are the main parameters in the diagnosis of uncomplicated myocardial contusion. The electrocardiogram is the "keystone" in the diagnostic armamentarium, as years of observation dictate. This opinion was previously noted by Christensen and Sutton, who concluded that the admission ECG was the most important diagnostic tool in the initial evaluation of patients with myocardial contusion and that 80% of the treatable cardiac arrhythmias were present at or shortly after admission to the emergency department.[10] Both must be done serially, that is, two or more times, depending on the patient's clinical status and place of observation (inpatient versus outpatient). Electrocardiographic changes, even the most subtle, can be of immense importance in the diagnosis and determination of possible risk for future events. The changes in myocardial depolarization (QRS complex) and repolarization (ST–T segments) can be of profound importance in the diagnosis or can be merely something that requires continued observation and serial testing. If they are accompanied by additional sites of cardiac injury, they become vastly more important. This also applies to their correlation with, and as a complement to, an abnormal echocardiogram or a high cardiac-specific enzyme abnormality. Currently, cardiac troponin I is the enzyme determination of choice.

Echocardiography can be a valuable supplement or necessary complement in the diagnosis of the various pathologic conditions that can arise from blunt cardiac trauma. Uncomplicated contusion can reveal varying degrees of muscular hypokinesia or dyskinesia, and akinesia in cases of moderate to severe contusion. It is especially effective for the evaluation of valve trauma resulting in valvular insufficiency, ruptured ventricular or atrial septa, pericardial effusion, aneurysmal formation, and pseudoaneurysms and as a gross evaluation of myocardial function (ejection fraction) in the absence of valvular insufficiency. It can also be of assistance in assessing the supravalvular area for evidence of a dissecting ascending aortic aneurysm.

Plain chest radiography would offer few diagnostic rewards in terms of myocardial contusion except in the presence of massive pericardial effusion, acute cardiac failure, or, in some cases, aneurysmal formation.

Cardiac troponin assay (preferably troponin I), can be a long-lived marker for cardiac injury, as long as seven or more days, thus making it useful for including or excluding a late diagnosis of serious myocardial trauma. Troponin assays have become more refined and are more specific and sensitive than when originally introduced. A troponin assay is invaluable in making a diagnosis of severe cardiac trauma or, equally so, its absence. It alleviates the frequent confusion resulting from the performance of other enzymes (i.e., CK-MB, myoglobin).[11,12]

Although still an emerging controversy, cardiac troponin assays are an invaluable addition in formulating necessary positive or negative diagnostic opinions for the purpose of assessing myocardial injury.[13]

Computerized tomography (CT) scans would be of much greater value in the assessment and detection of aortic aneurysms with or without dissection or in cases of dissection without aneurysmal formation.

Cardiac catheterization may be necessary to exclude suspected coronary occlusion associated with its rarely encountered traumatic coronary arterial injury or, equally as rare, posttraumatic stress insult that generally occurs within 1 to 2 hours postincident, and, certainly, less than 24 hours postincident.

Data is beginning to accumulate on the use of **cardiac enzymes** in the diagnosis of cardiac contusion. Some authors feel that they are of limited value, whereas others stress their importance for various reasons, not the least of which are the medical–legal concerns. It is opined that they are absolutely necessary, not merely to assist in making a diagnosis, but equally as important if not more so, to avoid the legal complications that frequently occur following blunt cardiac trauma. A review of the literature tends to suggest the preference for cardiac troponin I (cTnI) for this purpose. Cardiac troponin T (cTnT) may be expressed by other tissues in small quantity, but not nearly as much as creatine kinase MB (CK-MB), therefore making cTnI more specific under these circumstances. Recent studies have shown that even troponin I levels may become abnormal in patients with renal failure and heart failure and in some patients with myocardial ischemia of the noninfarctional type. The CK-MB isoenzyme can be considerably elevated in the presence of diffuse or severe muscular injury, as well as injuries to the brain, kidneys, and liver. Ischemic myocardial injury is associated with a greater degree of sensitivity for all cardiac enzymes when compared to myocardial contusion. This includes cTnI. The cardiac troponins have the advantage of sometimes remaining elevated for up to 1 week or longer following myocardial injury or infarction. They therefore become invaluable in making a delayed diagnosis of myocardial injury.

Controversy not withstanding, the greater specificity of cTnI makes it the preferable choice in cases of traumatic myocardial injury. Its sensitivity in these situations has not as yet been fully elucidated, but its presence can be helpful in alerting one to a diagnosis of myocardial contusion, and, most certainly, its absence would favor the exclusion of severe cardiac contusion. A complete classification of blunt cardiac trauma as proposed by RuDusky is valuable in terms of medical and legal definition (Table 3.4).

Table 3.4 Classification of Myocardial Contusion and Blunt Cardiac Trauma

Stage 0 (suspect)
No cardiac symptoms
No cardiac arrhythmias other than mild sinus tachycardia
No ECG abnormalities (normal ECG or unchanged from previous by comparison)
No elevation or slight elevation (borderline) of cardiac enzymes (cardiac troponin I or T)
No echocardiographic abnormality
No scintographic abnormality
Normal chest x-ray
No residual sequelae
Stage I (mild)
Minimal cardiac symptoms of brief duration and limited extent, (angina-like chest pain, atypical chest pain, palpitations)
No arrhythmias other than sinus tachycardia and atrial or ventricular extrasystoles
Minimal, transitory changes of ST segments or T waves on electrocardiogram (repolarization, ischemic, pericardial)
Unequivocal mild degree of elevation of cardiac enzymes
No echocardiographic abnormality
No scintographic abnormality
Normal chest x-ray
No residual or permanent sequelae
Stage II (moderate)
Significant or protracted cardiac chest pain
Marked sinus tachycardia
Frequent premature atrial or ventricular extrasystoles
Supraventricular arrhythmia either transitory and self-limited or requiring minimal intervention
Significant and more persistent ST-T wave abnormalities of several days' duration or longer (repolarization, ischemic, pericardial)
Moderate, significant elevation of cardiac enzymes
Echocardiographic evidence of mild, temporary hypokinesia or dyskinesia; minimal pericardial effusion, if present

(*Continued*)

Table 3.4 (Continued)

Abnormal scintographic study
Signs of external trauma (fractured ribs, sternum) possibly revealed in chest x-ray
No permanent sequelae
Stage III (severe)
Severe intermittent or persistent cardiac chest pain
Marked, persistent sinus tachycardia
Supraventricular arrhythmia requiring aggressive therapy
Ventricular arrhythmia
Protracted, significant ST-T wave abnormalities (repolarization, ischemic, pericardial, injury current)
Markedly elevated cardiac enzymes, or moderate elevations of longer duration than expected
Grossly abnormal echocardiographic abnormalities: marked hypokinesia, dyskinesia, akinesia, pericardial effusion
Easily discernible, grossly abnormal scintographic study
Evidence for acute myocardial infarction resulting from primary muscle injury or secondary to coronary arterial injury (thrombosis, laceration)
Arteriovenous fistula
Pericardial laceration
Valvular disruption not requiring immediate medical or surgical therapy (annulus, leaflet, chordae)
Chest x-ray evidence of external and internal trauma (pleural effusion, pulmonary contusion, possible mild pulmonary vascular congestion)
Possible permanent or delayed serious sequelae
Stage IV (catastrophic)
Severe systemic signs and symptoms (cardiac, pulmonary, vascular)
Acute, severe valvular dysfunction requiring immediate medical or surgical intervention (papillary muscle, multiple chordae, severe valve disruption).
Herniation of heart through pericardial laceration with signs and symptoms of major vascular obstruction requiring immediate intervention
Pericardial tamponade
Acute, severe congestive heart failure requiring immediate, highly aggressive intervention
Ventricular or atrial septal rupture
Great vessel laceration
Myocardial aneurysm
Myocardial pseudoaneurysm
Myocardial rupture
Permanent sequelae or death highly probable

Source: From RuDusky, B.M., *Angiology* 58:610–613, 2007. With permission, SAGE Publications.

Myocardial concussion, usually called “commotio cordis” is an acute arrhythmic disturbance of the heart (cardiac arrest) caused by a sudden high-velocity blow to the precordium (e.g., baseball, hockey puck, karate kick, fist punch to the chest, high-velocity football hit, etc.) It can result in a near-death experience or, if not self-terminated or bystander terminated, sudden cardiac death. It is generally stated that there is no pathologic evidence of gross myocardial damage or cellular injury by microscopic examination, although blood cell extravasation has been noted rarely to be present between myocardial fibers without disruption of myocardial fibers or necrosis.[14,15] It has been speculated that these deaths are due to ventricular dysrhythmia induced by the traumatic shock to the heart during an electrically vulnerable phase of ventricular excitabiliby.[14,16] It occurs so suddenly that there is no time for study and evaluation unless it is postmortem or during postresuscitation hospitalization, when attempts are made to distinguish it from myocardial contusion.[16] Speculation prevails that sudden arrhythmic death may preclude the development of pathologic signs that would be associated with significant myocardial contusion.

Consequences of Blunt Cardiac Trauma

4

As previously stated, **myocardial contusion** is the commonest complication of blunt cardiac trauma resulting from blunt chest injuries. It is also appropriate to reiterate that it can be a significant diagnostic dilemma to the attending and consulting physicians,[9] due in part to the lack of specific diagnostic criteria. The combination of the history, physical examination, and clinical observation assessed in conjunction with the laboratory evidence is absolutely necessary to assist in making the diagnosis. The diagnosis becomes less complicated in patients who do not have preexisting heart disease and the resulting associated pathophysiologic abnormalities. As previously discussed, the symptoms, signs, and diagnostic criteria have a wide range of variability from none to highly significant.

This also holds true for the complications resulting from blunt cardiac trauma, which range from none to highly morbid and death-producing (see Table 3.4). The simplest lesion is a mild, myocardial bruise, undetectable by clinical and laboratory evaluation. This type of contusion results in no symptoms and has no sequelae. A moderate contusion may be associated with any of the symptoms previously discussed and no sequelae. The severe contusion becomes highly problematic, especially when associated with preexisting medical conditions or those associated with the generalized trauma resulting in injury to other body organs or parts. Blunt myocardial trauma most commonly produces a contusion (bruise) involving a portion of the ventricular musculature, either the right or left ventricle but more frequently the former because of its more anterior position, as also occurs in cases of atrial injury. These opinions are derived from the work of Parmley et al., whereby autopsy evidence revealed that right ventricular and right atrial rupture were more common than their left-sided counterparts.[17] It should be noted that the differences may be less than substantiated, as anterior injuries are most likely to occur in direct blunt trauma with or without marked compression, and posterior injuries can involve predominantly the left ventricle and atrium where these structures are compressed against the thoracic spine. Parmley et al.'s data also showed that the tricuspid and mitral valves were injured with equal frequency.

It is axiomatic that any structure of the heart or within the chest may be injured during blunt chest, nonpenetrating cardiac trauma. Myocardial injury may be productive of only contusion or may cause rupture or laceration of a free wall or the septae, or can result in aneurysmal formation of the wall or of any blood vessel, great or small. Other consequences of blunt cardiac trauma are injuries to the pericardium, valves, valvular supporting structures, coronary arteries, or veins; great vessel injury; or rupture. The latter injuries may result in aneurysm formation, thrombosis, or various anatomical fistulae.

Traumatic ventricular or **atrial aneurysms** may occur as a result of severe chest trauma with extensive myocardial contusion or as a result of massive myocardial infarction due to arterial occlusion caused by the injury—an extremely rare phenomenon.

Pseudoaneurysms may occur as a result of severe blunt cardiac trauma. They are produced by rupture or laceration of the myocardium, which is usually sealed by pericardium or in combination with clot and fibrous tissue formation. Their discovery merits immediate surgical intervention to diminish the proclivity for rupture, hemopericardium with cardiac tamponade, exsanquination, and sudden death. Aneurysm formation as a result of blunt cardiac trauma is rare, and pseudoaneurysm formation is substantially more rare.[18] The right ventricle and the atria are the commonest sites of rupture, whereas delayed rupture usually involves the left ventricle. Cardiac aneurysms are considerably more frequent following acute myocardial infarction secondary to coronary thrombotic disease. It is common knowledge that traumatic blunt cardiac rupture is usually fatal and is rarely diagnosed preoperatively.[19]

It is important to note two important rules or exceptions to the rules concerning posttraumatic cardiac rupture: It may occur after seemingly minor occurrences with no evidence of serious trauma, and it can be significantly delayed—hours to months.

Simultaneous ruptures of the pericardium, all cardiac chambers, and the thoracic aorta in a healthy teenage male who fell over a soccer goal-post with no evidence of serious trauma has been reported.[20] Delayed death has been reported from 8 days to as long as 9 months following blunt cardiac trauma producing rupture or aneurysm formation.[21,22] Correction of valvular abnormalities has occurred from as late as 12 to 46 years following blunt cardiac trauma.[23,24] The discussion as to medical therapy with close follow-up versus early elective repair of valvular injuries is not simple or straightforward in many cases, and is subject to considerable debate. The trend in the medical literature favors early elective repair for various reasons, principally the prevention of progression of myocardial dysfunction.

A **pericardial tear** (rupture) is almost always (although not universally) associated with other injury to the heart or major blood vessels. More often, a posttraumatic pericarditis with effusion is present and is usually of minor degree. If a laceration of the heart occurs, and the pericardium is intact, cardiac tamponade may ensue, and can be fatal with as little as 150 to 200 ml of blood in the pericardial sac, but 600 to 1000 ml has been known to accumulate more slowly, with varying degrees of symptoms, not necessitating the immediate life-saving pericardiocentesis. This procedure prevents the restricted entry of blood into the right heart as well as the associated mechanical interference to myocardial contractility. If the pericardial sac is lacerated due to the injury, serious tamponade is usually avoided, and the blood will leak into the pleural spaces, causing hemorrhagic pleurisy, which may necessitate thoracentesis, depending on the extent and location of the primary injury. It generally holds true that the more serious the cardiac injury, the more serious can be the pericardial injury. Fibrinous pericarditis, often with some degree of hemorrhage is the commonest result of blunt pericardial injury.

Vascular Abnormalities III

Coronary Arterial Afflictions

5

Introduction

Cardiovascular disease is the commonest cause of death in the United States. Although the statistics may not be absolutely accurate, sudden cardiac deaths are estimated to occur in the vicinity of 400,000 annually. This figure can decrease due to the enhanced cardiac care now more commonly given in terms of diagnosis and treatment, and can also increase due to the continually expanding lifespan of the female and male population. Accurate data concerning the cause of death and related conditions is difficult to obtain because of physician impropriety in accurately assessing the factors relating to terminal status and causation in a scientific manner. It is obvious that everyone dies because their heart ceases to beat, or their respiratory center ceases to function. Therefore, simple cardiopulmonary arrest is neither science nor medicine when describing the cause of death without entering a plausible diagnosis of what prompted the cardiopulmonary arrest.[1,2,5]

Coronary atherosclerotic disease accounts for a large majority of sudden deaths, in fact, more so than all of the other cardiac diseases combined. It is also the commonest factor involved in all-cause cardiac mortality. Other causes that can be implicated in cardiac death are hypertensive disease, valvular heart disease, and various forms of cardiomyopathy, acute myocarditis, numerous infections and inflammatory states, toxic influences upon heart function, and cardiac trauma.

Coronary Artery Disease

Coronary atherosclerosis and arteriosclerosis are the most common diseases affecting the coronary arterial system and the heart in general. Combined, they are called arterio-atherosclerosis, as they are frequently coexistent, especially in the elderly.

Arteriosclerosis simply means hardening of the arteries. It generally implies a stiffening of the arterial wall and calcification of the medial and elastic layers of the artery. It is generally the coexistence of hypertension or diabetes mellitus with the aging process that results in a progressive, concentric calcification of the arterial media and is often more pronounced in the peripheral arterial system than in the coronary arteries. Atherosclerosis of the coronary arteries involves a complexity of inflammatory and fibroproliferative changes in response to injury. The inciting injury as yet has not been fully defined and is believed to be inflammatory in nature. Responsible factors are of mechanical and genetic origin and are closely tied to the deposition or imbibition of circulating atherogenic lipoproteins within the arterial intima and the subsequent pathologic response in the medial layer containing smooth muscle. Uncomplicated arteriosclerosis is far less detrimental to the human heart, as it imposes far less life-threatening complications. It is commonly associated with the diabetic state, chronic renal failure, uncontrolled hypertension, uncommon hereditable disease states, and advanced aging. It is, however, most often associated with atherosclerosis, as one considerably affects the other regardless of causative origin. The complexity of atherosclerotic development involves lipid deposition, smooth muscle and fibrous proliferation, immune activation, endothelial dysfunction, inflammatory responses, coagulopathic dysfunction, plaque formation and disruption, calcification, and thrombus formation.

Current research is evaluating the possibility of infectious agents of various types in the propagation or aggravation of coronary atherosclerosis and thrombosis, as well as plaque rupture. The latter consequence is clearly related to unstable angina and acute myocardial infarction. These include viral and bacterial agents with recent emphasis on Heliobacter and Chlamydia organisms, although a previous report has shown a lack of association of *Heliobacter pylori* in patients with coronary artery disease and myocardial infarction.[25] Coronary thrombosis may or may not be the end result of the atherosclerotic occlusive process. Factors involved in its pathology include genetically predetermined states and numerous extraneous mechanisms and interactions. These include metabolic transformation, mechanical stresses, lipid dysregulation, biochemical dysfunction, disturbances in the coagulation system, endothelial dysfunction, toxic states, infectious agents, mechanical trauma, and various other primary disease states (Tables 5.1 and 5.2).

Coronary thrombosis, with or without plaque rupture, when reaching a critical level, may produce progressive or unstable angina pectoris or myocardial infarction. Embolization of disrupted plaque material and thrombus may occlude the microcirculatory system, thereby producing downstream coronary arterial insufficiency and myocardial dysfunction even in the absence of arterial obstruction of the larger arteries. Acute myocardial infarction may result from long-standing, progressive thrombosis in vessels critically occluded or, most often, as a result of acute plaque rupture that can also result in acute thrombus formation and further occlusion or coronary vasospasm. Both **plaque rupture** and **coronary vasospasm** are more common in coronary arteries affected with mild to moderate atheromatous occlusion, generally in the range of 30 to 70%. Arteries with critical occlusion

Table 5.1 Factors that Influence Arterial Function and Status

Atherosclerosis
Hyperlipidemia
Dyslipidemias
Hypertension
Hyperhomocysteinemia
Diabetes mellitus
Smoking
Obesity
Chemical toxins
Endocrine disturbances
Rheumatoid (collagen) diseases
Infectious agents
Neoplastic diseases
Radiation
Coagulopathic disorders
Mechanical stress
Hemodynamic shear stress
Arteriosclerosis
Aging

Source: From RuDusky, B.M., *Angiology*, 53:503–507, 2002. With permission, SAGE Publications.

of 90% or greater usually occlude because of progressive thrombotic occlusion and never by coronary vasospasm, as vessels with that degree of stenosis are generally incapable of any significant vasospasm.

Plaque formation is highly dependent upon lipid metabolism and regulation; however, other factors share in this process. It is well known that a significant proportion of young individuals who have suffered a myocardial infarction have normal lipid studies. Various lipid subfractions are presently being given high-priority research, as are homocysteine level and inflammatory states other than that produced by plaques with a lipid-rich core.

Inflammatory changes, disruption of the fibrous cap of a lipid-rich plaque by mechanical and hemodynamic stress factors, and increased intra-endothelial pressure from accumulating "soft lipids" all can be involved in producing surface breaks in the intima or in the collagen-containing cap. This results in a hematologic attempt at sealing the tear or plaque rupture with extrusion of the lipid core material and extensive thrombus formation. Tears in the plaque surface induce the basic initial physiologic attempt of the reparative process—platelet adhesion, activation, and aggregation. The sum total of the basic atheromatous process thereby affects the vascular endothelium, intima, and media of the involved vessels in a highly complex fashion

Table 5.2 Biochemical Factors Involved in Coronary Arterial Function

Adenosine phosphates (AMP, ADP,ATP)
Prostacyclin
Thromboxane
Nitric oxide
Plasminogen activator system
HMG - coenzyme A
Protein kinase C
Adhesion molecules (selectins, integrins)
Cytoskelatal elements (F-actin collagen, elastin)
Cytosols
Phosphoinositide
Cytokines (interleukin, endothelin, bradykinin)
Hyperpolarizing factor
Collagenase
Elastase
Interferons (lymphokines)
Lipoprotein lipase
Platelet-derived growth factor
Transforming growth factor
Tumor necrosis factor alpha
Cholesterol ester transfer protein
Monocyte chemotactic protein
Calcium, sodium, potassium electrolyte system
Heparinoids
Angiotension II
Immune complexes
Neurohormonal factors (epinephrines, cortisol, dopamine, serotonin, histamine, other neuropeptides)
Hydroxyl and superoxide radicals
Antioxidants and vitamins (A, B, C, E)
Antithrombin III
von Willebrand factor
Insulin (?)
Other neurohormonal and enzymatic factors

Source: From RuDusky, B.M., *Angiology*, 53:503–507, 2002. With permission, SAGE Publications.

(Table 5.2). Activated and aggregated platelets produce what is known as the white clot. The continued coagulopathic process results in adherence of red blood cells and fibrin deposition, producing the so-called red clot or thrombus. Subsequently, vasoconstriction can further aggravate the occlusive process and vice versa. Endothelial function and the clotting cascade are quite intricately complex and involve numerous physiopharmacologic and biochemical interactions, with thrombin playing a critical role.

Symptoms produced by occlusive coronary arterial disease vary considerably among individual patients and are dependent upon the extent, location, and number of coronary lesions, as well as the presence of collateral circulation and individual patient characteristics. The commonest symptom is **angina pectoris** (chest pain), variously described as a feeling of chest tightness, heaviness, pressure, burning, or squeezing, which may radiate to one or both sides of the neck or jaw, down one or both arms, or to the interscapular area of the back. Radiation of pain to other sites has been described but is uncommon. Often overlooked by both patient and physician, an anginal equivalent may be present (symptoms without true chest pain). This is usually described as a sensation of being short of breath (breathlessness), generally on performing certain physical activities, including simple walking beyond a specific distance, walking up one or more flights of stairs or carrying heavy packages.

In most cases an obstruction of 75% or greater is present in one or more major coronary arteries or branch vessels. Vasospastic angina can occur under the influence of excess emotional or physical stress with far less severe lesions, and may also occur in patients with normal coronary arteries. Coronary arterial vasospasm is also seen in patients with **Prinzmetal's angina**, which often occurs at rest, and in patients with either normal coronary arteries or varying degrees of focal stenosis.

An ECG taken during these episodes of Prinzmetal's angina reveals S-T segment elevation compatible with acute current of injury, and is normal when these episodes of chest pain are not present. This is in sharp contrast to the ECG changes involved in acute or chronic ischemic angina, which reveal ST and T wave depression or negativity.

Congenital abnormalities of the coronary arteries are known to produce symptoms of anginal chest distress and are often a previously undiagnosed cause of sudden death, defined only at autopsy. The commonest congenital abnormality encountered involves the abnormal origin of a coronary artery (malformation). This may produce myocardial impairment due to inadequate coronary arterial blood supply to the affected ventricle. Sudden cardiac death in a 16-year-old male while playing recreational basketball, due to anomalous congenital origin of both coronary arteries, has been described and its incidence discussed in detail by Catanzaro et al.[26] Other conditions not considered rarities are hypoplasia of a main coronary artery or its dominant branches, fibrous dysplasia, and aneurysmal formation, which can be congenital or acquired. All may lead to subsequent ischemic episodes and may produce sudden death if undiagnosed during a symptom-producing stage. **Congenital aneurysms** of the coronary artery most commonly occur in the right coronary artery and occur in about 1.5% of the patient population.[27]

Less frequent are **coronary artery fistulae**, which are an abnormal communication between a major epicardial artery and a cardiac chamber or another vessel. They may be congenital or acquired and are said to occur in approximately 0.1% of patients.[28]

Myocardial bridging is less commonly diagnosed, and may be overlooked at the time of cardiac catheterization. It can be a source of significant clinical symptoms, depending on its location and extent. It occurs as an anatomical variation in the distribution or location of a coronary artery as it passes through a specific segment of myocardium, whereby it is compressed or temporarily occluded during systolic contraction of the heart. Myocardial bridging is said to occur in 5 to 80% of patients at necropsy and in 0.5 to 12% of patients undergoing cardiac catheterization. The complicating factors of anatomic distribution are relevant to the severity of symptoms and their eventual outcome.

Dissection of a coronary artery can occur in association with various primary disease states affecting the artery or can be secondary to arterial trauma of various types and origins. The latter include radiation exposure, lightning strikes, blunt chest trauma, iatrogenically-induced medical (procedural) trauma, and spontaneous dissection of idiopathic origin. There is an increased incidence of **spontaneous coronary artery dissection in females** (with or without association with coronary artery aneurysms) during the **peripartum period of pregnancy**. These cases can have tragic outcomes as a result of massive myocardial infarction, cardiac arrhythmia, and sudden death.

Direct injury to a coronary artery may occur as a result of blunt chest trauma, but this is the exception rather than the rule. When it does occur, the left anterior descending coronary artery is most likely to be involved because of its anatomic location. Coronary arteries that are atherosclerotic are more susceptible to the side effects of blunt cardiac trauma. The resultant effects are thrombosis, hemorrhage, dissection, aneurysm formation, or frank rupture. The pathophysiologic clinical result can be myocardial ischemia or infarction and the various complications that may arise from either insult.

Coronary artery ectasia is a degenerative state of an epicardial coronary artery, singularly or in combination, often associated with ascending aortic aneurysms or abdominal aortic aneurysms. They may be associated with atherosclerosis, genetic defects, or inflammatory disease states. Coronary ectasia may lead to aneurysmal development, dissection, and obstruction. **True aneurysms of the coronary circulation** are always associated with severe atherosclerosis, in contrast to coronary ectasia, which may be completely free of atherosclerosis.

Vascular Injury

6

Depending on the extent, location, and severity of the trauma, any blood vessel in the chest or abdomen or any combination thereof may be involved in some type of vascular injury. Partial tears, transmural tears, and contusion without tears may contribute to hemorrhage, thrombosis, vasculitus, aneurysm, and pseudoaneurysm formation. Compression and deceleration forces similar to those producing direct or indirect cardiac injury are involved. The most frequent vessel involved is the aorta. Venous structures are less commonly involved. Injuries to the thoracic aorta are the commonest great vessel blunt injury. The innominate, subclavian, or carotid arteries may be involved, as well as the superior vena cava. The commonest site of rupture is the area of the aortic isthmus, just distal to the origin of the left subclavian artery. The most common site involved is the ascending aorta, and in these patients concomitant cardiac injury commonly occurs. Probably fewer than 20% of patients survive aortic rupture, and those that survive surgical correction are frequently left with comorbid conditions, including varying degrees of cerebral dysfunction. The preinjury status of a patient's cerebral function is a definite contributing factor to the end result, which is usually influenced by the degree and duration of the shock syndrome with its accompanying decrease in cerebral perfusion.

Lacerations of the aorta may occur in association with many different types of trauma but are usually the result of automotive accidents of all types, regardless of the location of impact. The root of the aorta may be lacerated and can produce a sudden, fatal hemopericardium, or it may be completely torn from the base of the heart. The tears may be partial or complete and may or may not be associated with aortic dissection. As is generally accepted, an atherosclerotic aorta is more prone to laceration and dissection than is a healthy aorta. The attachment of the ligamentum arteriosum, which fixates the aorta to its intrathoracic position, serves as an excellent fulcrum for kinetic force. Death may be nearly instantaneous or delayed, depending on the type of laceration and its location. It is commonly accepted that most aortic injuries lead to a rapid demise, but delayed complications are known to occur, and in these situations death may be preventable by rapid diagnosis and surgical intervention. Most of these cases are associated with hematoma formation, false aneurysm formation, or posttraumatic dissection.

A **false aneurysm** of the aorta may develop following aortic rupture. This is most frequently seen in patients who had gone undiagnosed or required no immediate surgical intervention. These false aneurysms may not be discovered for months or years following blunt chest trauma.

Clinically, the diagnosis of aortic rupture with or without dissection should be suspected in a patient complaining of severe, lancinating pain in the chest or interscapular area. The pain may be accompanied by high blood pressure in the arms and a widened pulse pressure. These may occur at a significant time interval prior to the development of the shock syndrome, at which time the patient becomes moribund. A widened mediastinal silhouette on the plain chest film should prompt the physician to make a rapid diagnosis by means of transesophageal echocardiography (TEE) or computerized tomography (CT) scan of the chest. Immediate surgical intervention is the rule if survival is to be expected.

Abdominal vascular injury is often associated with trauma to one or more abdominal viscera, but in certain instances can be the only injury to occur. Sometimes there may be little or no external evidence of trauma. The forensic specialist must take into account other pathologic states that are known to produce aneurysmal formation or spontaneous rupture. Those most frequently encountered are cystic medial necrosis of the aorta, atherosclerosis, syphilis, and localized arteritis from whatever cause. Clues pointing toward the need for more intensive evaluation and observation in order to diagnose the possible presence of intrathoracic cardiovascular injury are rib or sternal fractures and fracture-dislocations of the vertebrae.

Iatrogenic trauma to intrathoracic structures is becoming more common with the advent of numerous invasive technologic procedures used for diagnostic purposes and therapy. Arterial and venous perforation secondary to the use of various types of catheters during these procedures is not uncommon. Cardiac perforation can also occur and may be associated with a spectrum of minimal to disastrous consequences. Coronary arterial injury with perforation or dissection is now commonplace in association with coronary angioplasty, stent placement, and other technical procedures in the treatment of coronary occlusion.

One must also be aware that with the continually increasing use of anticoagulants of all types, complications of intracavitary hemorrhage, intracerebral bleeds, organ hemorrhage, and spontaneous intramuscular hemorrhage have become more frequent.

7 Aortic Aneurysms and Aortic Dissection

Important and dramatic as blunt aortic injuries are, nontraumatic aortic disease can be equally so. The forensic specialist must take into account other pathologic states that are known to affect the aorta and can lead to aneurysmal formation or spontaneous rupture with or without dissection. Those most frequently encountered are cystic medial necrosis, atherosclerosis, syphilis, and localized arteritis of varying etiologies. Cocaine-related thoracic aortic dissection has also been reported.[29,30]

Factors that predispose to dissection include hypertension, diabetes, pregnancy, smoking, hyperlipidemia, congenital aortic valve disease, connective tissue diseases, and blunt and penetrating injuries that were unrecognized following the initial insult.

Clinical symptoms and signs vary according to the location of the dissection and branch arterial vessel involvement. Pain—sudden and strikingly sharp, tearing, stabbing, or lancinating—is the hallmark of initial symptomatology. It can be anteriorly or posteriorly predominant in the thorax or abdomen.

Signs or symptoms of stroke syndromes may occur because of carotid or vertebral occlusion when the thoracic aorta is involved, and those of myocardial infarction may occur due to coronary ostial occlusion. In abdominal dissection, ischemic bowel necrosis or renal insufficiency can occur, as well as arterial occlusive disease to the lower extremities.

The symptom and sign complexes in cases of **thoracic aortic aneurysms** often overlap, but mostly depend on the type of dissection and its relationship to the location and the extent of the dissection. The infrequently used classification of types I, II, and III thoracic aortic dissections has now been largely replaced by type A and type B. In the former classification, type I referred to dissection of the entire thoracic aorta (proximal to distal), type II involved only the proximal or ascending aorta to the arch, and type III involved the descending thoracic aorta. The more commonly used type A includes the old types I and II and are now called proximal or ascending dissection, and type B is the old type III, now called distal (which can include the arch) or descending thoracic dissection. More than 80% of type A dissections begin in the proximal portion of the ascending aorta, and in type B dissections, a similar frequency begins in the mid- to distal arch.

In particular, patients with hereditary connective-tissue disorders (Marfan's syndrome and Ehlers-Danlos syndrome) are prone to progressive medial degeneration and ultimate dissection, usually affecting the proximal aorta (type A dissection). Ominous clinical signs are pulsus paradoxus, jugular neck vein distension, pericardial friction rub, and hypotension, suggesting pericardial tamponade or extensive dissection with or without rupture. The commonest cause of death in patients with proximal dissection of the ascending aorta is cardiac tamponade, whereas in the case of abdominal aneurysms, the commonest cause of death is blood loss and hypovolemic shock.

The incidence of aortic dissection has been found to vary from 3 to 4 per 100,000 individuals per year, with at least 36% prehospital mortality. The ratio of proximal to distal thoracic dissection varies from 2:1 to 5:1.[31]

Diagnostic considerations are routine radiography, emergent echocardiography, abdominal ultrasound, CT scanning, and MRI. The routine chest x-ray can be normal or can reveal aortic or mediastinal widening or various irregularities in the aortic contour. If immediately available, transesophageal echocardiography is the immediate or urgent diagnostic procedure of choice for detecting aneurysms of the ascending aorta and is optimal for evaluating the unstable patient. Abdominal ultrasound may reveal aneurysmal dilatation, but CT or MRI scanning are the procedures of choice. CT scanning and aortograhy both have sensitivities and specificities of 90% and 95%, respectively. Aortography is more time-consuming but is valuable in detecting coronary occlusion and in defining the branch vessels, which may be involved. Magnetic resonance imaging is said to have 99% sensitivity and specificity but also is time-consuming, and is not always immediately available. Transesophageal echocardiography (TEE) has a similar sensitivity but less specificity in the evaluation of thoracic aortic dissection.

In the evaluation of thoracic aortic dissection, Nienaber et al. found MRI and TEE to be 100% sensitive in any dissection of the thoracic aorta, with a specificity of 100% and 68%, respectively. The TEE approach had a lower specificity due to false positive findings in the ascending aorta.[32] MRI was superior in the detection of thrombus formation in a false lumen, and there was no demonstrable difference in the detection of pericardial effusion, aortic insufficiency, or the site of the dissection. The decreased sensitivity of TEE was predominantly due to failure of detection of abnormalities in the ascending aorta because of extensive plaque formation, aortic ectasia, aortic injury, or previous surgery. MRI took up to four times longer to perform than TEE, an important logistic triage consideration, especially in unstable patients. If possible (time and clinical status permitting), MRI should still be performed prior to surgery to completely assess the extent of aortic involvement and the intricacies associated with them. The recent developments in MRI scanning have made it the procedure of choice for many individuals, but one must be cautious of its time-consuming use in cases of unstable patients, as well as in patients with pacemakers, prosthetic valves, surgical clips, and so on.

The management of these patients is also a source of controversy, but in unstable patients and those with acute dissection of the ascending aorta, immediate surgery should be undertaken. Dissection of the aortic arch and distal thoracic aorta can often be medically managed initially unless there are imposing and evident complications.

It has been suggested that an elevated d-dimer level may be of considerable value in the initial assessment of patients with chest pain who were subsequently diagnosed as having acute dissection of the thoracic aorta.[33] The sensitivity was found to be 100% in 24 patients, making the diagnosis of thoracic aortic dissection unlikely in the presence of a negative test.

Observational follow-up evaluation is dependent upon the aneurysm, its location and extent, and the individual patient. Age, physical and mental status, and numerous comorbid conditions must be taken into account. Surgery is generally not recommended in asymptomatic patients who have aneurysms of less than 5 cm in greatest diameter. Aneurysmal dilation of 5-cm diameter is the so-called "bite the bullet zone," in which case watchful waiting may be appropriate. The danger zone is 6-cm diameter, especially for thoracic aortic aneurysms, and 7 cm is the "disaster soon to follow" zone. Blood pressure control is of paramount importance. It is often stated that aneurysms increasing in diameter by 0.5 cm per year should receive careful observation and undergo measurement by the selected means every 6 months. This is generally ultrasound in the case of abdominal aortic aneurysms and CT scan in thoracic aneurysms.

The more recently introduced techniques of stent grafting of abdominal and descending thoracic aortic aneurysms offer greater promise to the more critically ill patients who suffer from various confounding comorbidities.[34]

Complications known to occur with stent grafting are renal failure, bowel ischemia and infarction, paraplegia, embolism, infection, graft fracture or leaks, and rupture of the aneurysm.

Patients with acute proximal thoracic aortic dissection require immediate surgery, whereas a distal (descending) dissection, if uncomplicated, allows one to have the necessary time for medical management and further contemplation of the therapeutic course to follow. Since the advent of CT and MRI scanning, two additional pathologic entities have been described: penetrating aortic ulcers and intramural hematomas.[31] These were rarely diagnosed in the earlier angiographic era. Ulceration may lead to hematoma formation or dissection. Future research may shed light on the possibility of decreasing the incidence of these lesions by the use of statin therapy to enhance antilipemic effects and the proposed anti-inflammatory and endothelial healing factors involved with such therapy. Contrary to popular opinion, especially that of plaintiff's attorneys, the majority of patients do not give a history of strenuous physical activity prior to dissection, except the few who have engaged in weight lifting, whereby a severe hypertensive response occurs due to the isometric physiologic effect of such exercise. Patients with Marfan's syndrome and other connective tissue disorders should be followed at least on an annual basis, and when the diameter of the aortic root approaches a ratio of 1.3 above normal dimension, follow-up should be shortened to every 6 months. Elective repair is generally considered with ratios above this range because of the high risk of dissection.

Although medical therapy is generally considered to be the primary therapy of choice for uncomplicated dissection of the arch or descending aorta, it may also be the only therapy appropriate for patients with ascending aortic dissection who suffer from various combinations of serious comorbidities. Under those circumstances very few patients who sustain multiple complications survive. The introduction and development of aortic-stenting will undoubtedly change the overall management of these cases, as well as the mortality statistics. In uncomplicated cases, the operative mortality ranges from 5 to 30%, and in complicated cases from 25 to 60% or higher, especially in patients with type B dissection. The mortality rate for untreated thoracic aortic dissection is at least 50% within the first 2 days, and patients with type A dissection invariably require immediate surgical repair. In some institutions, surgical repair is not advocated for uncomplicated cases of type B dissection, with an operative mortality as low as 10%.[35]

Regardless of the initial or subsequent mode of therapy, patients who survive aortic dissection are considered to be lifelong candidates for medical therapy. In addition to the basic aortic aneurysm or dissection repair in patients with type A dissection, aortic valve reconstruction or replacement is often necessary, the latter especially so in patients with Marfan's syndrome or other connective tissue disorders. The survival rate at 1 month after medical therapy is stated as being 43% in patients with type A dissection, compared to 91% of those with type B dissection. After 5 years, life expectancy rates are diminished by approximately 10 years in patients with type A dissection and can approach normal in patients with type B dissection. The reoperative rate can vary from 15 to 30% over a period of 5 to 10 years after surgery.

Thoracic and thoracoabdominal aortic aneurysms can be classified as hereditable in patients with Marfan's syndrome, Ehlers-Danlos syndrome, and so on. These conditions may also produce **annulo-aortic ectasia**, a degeneration of the fibrous component of the aorta, which causes dilation of the annulus, proximal ascending aorta, and sinuses of Valsalva. It may also be associated with valvular abnormalities, predominantly mitral, and can lead to aortic insufficiency and dissection of the aorta. Similar pathologic conditions may be produced by arteriosclerotic degenerative vascular disease or inflammatory states producing aortitis due to various pathogens, autoimmune disorders, and radiation injury. In patients undergoing surgery for ascending aortic aneurysms, Papadakis et al. found a 25.6% incidence of coronary artery ectasia (CAE). Most cases are associated with coronary atherosclerosis, but it has been found in patients with vascular ectasia in peripheral arteries, the pulmonary artery, and the venous system and with ectasia of the abdominal aorta.[36]

Penetrating aortic ulcers are a complication of atheromatous-degenerative plaques that erode into the vessel wall, producing hematoma formation, pseudoaneurysms, frank rupture, or aortic dissection. They may produce subjective symptoms similar to those of dissection, may be difficult to diagnose, and should be considered to be an ominous portent of future catastrophic events and require immediate medical therapy and, in most cases, urgent surgical intervention. Aortic atheromata and ulcers lead to the formation of aortic thrombi, a frequent source of distal embolization to the arteries of the brain, the abdominal viscera, and the upper and lower extremities. **Floating thrombi** in the ascending aorta have been described and are a source of life-threatening stroke and peripheral embolization leading to gangrene and limb loss.[37] When discovered, immediate intervention is necessary, usually surgical.

Cogert and Siegel reported a giant floating aortic thrombus following an aortic injury due to a motor vehicle accident. They concluded that transesophageal echocardiography should be considered in patients who have sustained blunt aortic trauma.

When unassociated with degenerative and inflammatory disease states or trauma, aortic dissection in young individuals commonly occurs secondary to cocaine use. Its production is influenced by the abrupt severe hypertension, cateclolamine release, and tachycardia associated with **cocaine abuse**. Underlying (undiagnosed) pathology allows the condition to occur more easily. Chronic cocaine use may be accompanied by injury to blood vessels and cardiac muscle and may contribute to the acceleration of atherosclerosis.[29] The use of crack cocaine may contribute more significantly to the development of acute aortic dissection.[30]

A most difficult diagnostic dilemma is the presence of **painless acute thoracic aortic dissection** associated with both type A and B dissections. The mortality was higher in patients with type B dissection (43% vs. 10.4%).[38] The clinical characteristics of the patients in this study are noted in Table 7.1.

Abdominal aortic aneurysms (AAAs) are commonly found on routine testing and clinical evaluation. The highest incidence is predominantly found in males over 65 years of age. Approximately 5% of this population will have an abdominal aortic aneurysm (defined as 3 cm in diameter or greater). They are generally asymptomatic until they begin to tear or rupture. There is a 75% or greater mortality following rupture. Most abdominal aortic aneurysms are located in the infrarenal portion of the aorta. There is still considerable debate as to their mechanism of production. Some investigators believe that underlying genetic factors are mostly responsible, while others believe the aging process associated with degeneration of the media and with

Table 7.1 Clinical Characteristics of Patients with Painless Thoracic AAD[a]

Characteristics	Group 1 (painless AAD)	Group 2 (painful AAD)	*p* value
	Dissection		
Type A (ascending aorta or arch)	47 (74.6)	557 (60.9)	.03
Type B (descending aorta)	16 (25.4)	357 (39.1)	
	Demographic		
Mean ± SD age (y)	66.6 ± 13.3	61.9 ± 14.1	.01
Male	39 (61.9)	626 (68.5)	.27
	Previous medical history		
Atherosclerosis	24 (39.3)	250 (28.2)	.06
Diabetes	6 (10.2)	35 (4.0)	.04
Aortic aneurysm	18 (29.5)	116 (13.1)	<.001
Prior cardiovascular surgery[b]	24 (39.3)	126 (14.9)	<.001
	Presenting symptom and sign		
Syncope	21 (33.9)	105 (11.7)	<.001
Stroke	7 (11.3)	42 (4.7)	.03
Other neurologic deficit	5 (8.1)	91 (10.2)	.59
Congestive heart failure	12 (19.7)	34 (3.9)	<.001
Fever	2 (8.0)	20 (4.3)	.31
Murmur of aortic insufficiency	21 (40.4)	276 (32.7)	.25
Pulse deficits	11 (22.0)	223 (27.8)	.37
Pericardial friction rub	2 (3.4)	12 (1.4)	.22
	Blood pressure		
Hypertensive	19 (33.9)	424 (48.2)	.04
Normotensive	29 (52.7)	328 (37.1)	.02
Hypotensive	5 (8.6)	98 (11.1)	.56
Shock or cardiac tamponade	8 (13.6)	95 (10.6)	.48

Source: From Park, S.W., Hutchinson, S., Kim, N.H., et al., *Mayo Cl. Proc.*, 79:1252-1257, 2004. With permission.

[a] Values are numbers (percentage) unless indicated otherwise. AAD = acute aortic dissection.

[b] Includes aortic valve or mitral valve surgery and coronary artery bypass grafting.

atherosclerosis are the principle mechanisms involved in the development of aneurysmal formation.

Nevertheless, inflammatory mechanisms are considered to be associated with the production of AAAs and various pathogens including viruses have been found in 27 to 65% of specimens.[39] This does not, however, define the role of these pathogens in the pathogenesis of aneurysms. Although genetic factors must be implicated in the pathogenesis of AAAs, the predominate risk factors are age, smoking, atherosclerosis, and hypertension. Disease states such as Marfan's syndrome, Ehlers-Danlos syndrome, connective tissue disease, cystic medial necrosis, and so on are categorized separately as distinct entities that are shown to have a special predilection for aneurysmal development. In an attempt to answer the question "Is aortic dilation an atherosclerosis-related process?", Agmon, et al., concluded that age, gender (male), and body surface area are major determinants of thoracic aortic dimensions and that risk factors for atherosclerosis and atherosclerotic plaques are weak determinants for the prevalence of distal thoracic aortic aneurysmal formation in the general population.[40]

A combined veterans' hospital study found an incidence of abdominal aortic aneurysms of 4.0 cm or larger in size in 1.4% of the population studied. The excess prevalence associated with smoking accounted for 78% of the patient sample. The researchers concluded that smoking is the risk factor most strongly associated with abdominal aortic aneurysms.[41]

The symptoms and signs that can be associated with a **complicated abdominal aortic aneurysm** are legion. Except in cases of the more obvious abdominal catastrophic events, which occur as a result of dissection or rupture, suspicion is most often the key to a prompt diagnosis and avoidance of a catastrophic outcome. It is the noncatastrophic case that is more likely to be missed, as the symptoms are often mistaken for the more common and less urgent intra-abdominal problems. These symptoms are often associated with every abdominal organ and site: stomach, intestines, spleen, kidneys, pancreas, nonaortic vasculature, and bladder. In the female, pathology of the ovaries and uterus may add to the confusion.

The **symptoms and signs of an expanding, tearing or ruptured abdominal aortic aneurysm** vary according to the state of the disease, the size and location of the pathology, and the inherent pain response of the individual patient. Ruptured aneurysms with hypotension and shock are those most frequently diagnosed in the emergency room. The symptom associated with ruptured and unruptured aneurysms is generally pain, found in 83% or more of patients with some type of rupture or tear. Pain associated with unruptured aneurysms is a signal of expansion or partial disruption of the vessel wall. In patients in whom the rupture involves the retroperitoneal space, the blood may be contained for many hours or even weeks before a hemorrhagic hypotensive catastrophe occurs. In the earlier phase, urinary symptoms such as retention, abdominal spasms, and flank pain may occur. Constipation and localized tenderness may be found, adding confusion to the diagnosis and relating it to renal, genitourinary, or intestinal problems. Obtaining an immediate ultrasound of the abdomen may point one in the right direction and lead to the usually necessary CT scan of the abdomen. It should be remembered, however, that a CT scan that does not reveal leakage should not be considered a rejection of the aneurysmal cause of the patient's symptoms.

The issue of the elective repair of small, asymptomatic abdominal aneurysms remains open to question and often depends on factors such as geographic area, individual preference and experience, concomitant comorbidities, and individual patient acceptance or preference. A United Kingdom study found no long-term difference in mean survival between the early-surgery and surveillance groups, but after 8 years the total mortality was lower in the early-surgery group. The researchers felt that the difference could be attributed to the beneficial changes in lifestyle adopted by members of the early-surgery group.[42] Similarly, the Veterans Affairs cooperative study group concluded that survival is not improved by elective repair of abdominal aortic aneurysms smaller than 5.5 cm even when operative mortality is low.[43]

There is increasing evidence that lipid-lowering therapy (i.e., statins) can result in a reduction in the size, quality, and number of atheromatous plaques in various arterial systems. This was noted to be especially prevalent in the thoracic aorta, and can occur after 12 months of therapy. It was less prevalent in the abdominal aorta, in which cases age was a confounding factor in the results obtained from therapy.[43]

Iatrogenic dissection of the **thoracic and abdominal aorta** is becoming more frequent with the advances in and increased use of various diagnostic and therapeutic techniques. Aortic dissections may occur as a result of cardiac surgery, coronary arteriography, cardiac and peripheral vascular catheterization, vascular surgery, and stent placement. The overall incidence is not exactly known or yet appreciated. Type A aortic dissections were found to be more prevalent following cardiac surgery, and type B dissections more prevalent following coronary angiography or associated interventions.[44]

Pseudoaneurysm of a thoracic aortic graft secondary to puncture by fractured sternal wires has been reported, but unfortunately led to a fatal stroke outcome following a successful patch graft repair.[45] **Endograft failure** following stent placement for treatment of abdominal aortic aneurysms is a recognized complication of the procedure and has been described as a cause of late complications related to various types of mechanical trauma, including heavy exercise.[46]

In general, **abdominal aortic aneurysms** greater than 5.5 cm should be considered for **prophylactic repair** when applicable clinical situations and comorbidities are considered.

Nonpenetrating Vascular Injury

Nonpenetrating **traumatic vascular injury** can involve any artery or vein in any location of the body, depending on the type of injury, the location and extent of the trauma, the physical force involved, and the inherent status of the vessel.

It is usually the thoracic aorta that is involved in the multitude of possible injuries that can produce acute thoracic aortic rupture or disruption, the latter with or without dissection or pseudoaneurysm formation.

It has been estimated that up to 16% of serious traumatic accident victims (generally motor vehicle accidents) suffer **an injury to the thoracic aorta**, of which 80 to 90% die suddenly. Of the survivors, 40% rupture in less than 24 hours.[47] Most traumatic ruptures of the thoracic aorta occur at the isthmus near the attachment of the ligamentum arteriosum, followed by the supravalvular area and then the distal descending aorta.[48] The mechanisms involve combinations of varying physical and directional forces, arterial attachments, the normal variations in anatomic strength of aortic tissue at certain locations, the inherent state of each individual's aorta, and the intra-aortic pressure produced by the particular type of injury and its location.

Ruptures may be partial, involving the intima, media, or adventitia, or full thickness, involving all three layers of the involved artery. When the patient survives, the trauma may result in **pseudoaneurysm formation**, or over a variable period of time, true aneurysm formation may occur. Complete aortic transection (dehiscence) from its root is known to occur. Aortic rupture with concomitant transection of the left bronchus has also been reported.[49]

A difficult to diagnose complication of thoracic aortic dissection or aortic pseudoaneurysm is **occlusion of the left main coronary artery**. This situation can produce acute myocardial infarction or anginal chest distress, or can be asymptomatic. Electrocardiographic changes in the ST segments and T waves may offer a clue, and their presence may be further suspected from anatomic abnormalities on transesophageal echocardiography. Ultimately, a cardiac catheterization is usually necessary.[50,51] Aortic dissection following blunt chest trauma is considered to be an uncommon event. Clues on the chest x-ray may be suggestive of an aortic tear (Table 7.2).

As with the diagnosis of blunt cardiac trauma, a high index of suspicion is the foremost advantage in diagnosing blunt aortic trauma. Symptoms of thoracic aortic injury are similar to those of spontaneous aortic dissection and include chest pain, interscapular pain, dysphagia, hoarseness, dyspnea, stridor, and neurologic symptoms secondary to upper extremity ischemia,

Table 7.2 Radiographic Clues of a Thoracic Aortic Tear

Obliteration of the aortic knob
Widened mediastinum
Deviation of the trachea
Depressed left main bronchus
Hemothorax
Fracture of scapula, spine, or first or second ribs
Blunting of the sharp aortic outline
Shift of the esophagus (rightward)

spinal cord ischemia, or cerebral ischemia. For the few survivors of traumatic aortic rupture or transection, only immediate surgery offers any hope of survival, especially in those who immediately survive the transection. Those with rupture or tears may survive long enough to develop a false aneurysm and have more time for evaluation and emergency surgery. Angiography is recommended if the patient's condition is stable, and may be advised or precluded, depending on comorbid conditions and injuries. Catheter angiography has been largely replaced by CT and MRI angiography, generally the latter if it is immediately available. Transesophageal echocardiography if rapidly available and with expert interpretation can be helpful, especially in cases of proximal and distal descending thoracic aortic trauma. Its inability to provide adequate visualization of the distal ascending aorta and the proximal aorta are known limitations of its value.[52] Victims ejected from a vehicle are twice as likely to have aortic rupture than the driver or passenger not thrown from the vehicle.[53] The Duke experience up to 1990 noted that 21% of victims who sustained posttraumatic thoracic aortic aneurysms also had concomitant left ventricular contusion.[54]

Spontaneous rupture of the thoracic aorta has been rarely reported in the absence of aneurysm, dissection, trauma, medical degenerative states, inflammatory disease, or hypertension.[55] Fatal rupture of an unsuspected posttraumatic aneurysm of the thoracic aorta during pregnancy 15 years after an automobile accident as been reported.[56]

A case report from Canada described the successful treatment of an initially contained blunt traumatic aortic isthmus rupture with recurrence the following morning, using an endovascular stent graft.[57]

Not surprisingly, **traumatic rupture of the abdominal aorta** is less common than traumatic thoracic aortic rupture. Its suspicion, signs, and symptoms are those previously noted in the discussion of abdominal aortic aneurysms. It must be remembered, however, that no symptoms from a ruptured abdominal aorta need be present, especially in cases of severe associated trauma and hypotension or shock. **Abdominal aortic pseudoaneurysms** (AAP) following blunt trauma are rare, with less than 30 cases reported in the literature. Pseudoaneurysm formation more commonly involves the thoracic aorta. Most cases result from penetrating trauma such as gunshot or stab wounds. Repair of an AAP 15 years after an injury sustained in a car accident has been reported.[58]

Successful surgical management of a chronic dissection of an aneurysm of the left subclavian artery associated with pseudocoarctation of the aorta has been described.[59] The dissection was believed to be initiated by blunt trauma. Subclavian aneurysms are often associated with coarctation of the aorta. **Intrathoracic segmental subclavian artery aneurysms** may be secondary to trauma, infection, medial degeneration, or atherosclerosis.

Nontraumatic Vasculopathies

8

Spontaneous carotid artery dissection with stroke is generally a morbid event producing acute stroke symptoms with dysarthria and hemiparesis. The degree of impairment may vary from complete or near complete resolution to permanent and serious neurologic deficits. It is described as being "idiopathic" but is usually associated with intimal disease or medial degeneration. Its occurrence in association with various coagulopathic states is highly debatable, if not questionable.[60] It has been known to be initiated by blunt trauma, in which cases thrombotic occlusion may be associated with the dissection or may occur independently.

Peripartum coronary arterial dissection is a highly morbid condition usually occurring during the first 2 weeks postpartum. It is believed to be due to an enigmatic vasculitis and most often affects the left anterior descending coronary artery. Treatment involves a range of choices from medical, stenting, and surgical revascularization as determined by the clinical status, principally following the necessary cardiac catheterization. Multiple dissections have been known to occur but are rare.

Vertebral artery dissection may also be idiopathic or induced by blunt or other mechanical trauma, with or without other associated medical conditions. It is less common than internal carotid artery dissection, but both should be placed near the top of the differential diagnosis list in younger patients (less than 45 years) who present with a neurologic deficit or syndrome for unknown reasons or cause. Often, the simple presentation of headache, neck pain, and nuchal rigidity in a young person can be a clue to vertebral artery dissection or occlusion. Unfortunately, the diagnosis is usually not entertained or confirmed until the neurologic deficits become manifest. These may include numbness and tingling of the face and arms, dizziness, ataxia, hoarseness, and difficulty swallowing. Unilateral impairment of motor strength and coordination of the arm and leg may occur.

Chang et al.[61] reported a case of **spontaneous bilateral vertebral artery dissection** in a 29-year-old male. The pathophysiology of dissection includes hemorrhage, thrombosis, and embolism with resultant partial or complete occlusion of a vessel, resulting in cerebral ischemia of varying degree and location. They noted that causative mechanisms have included head and neck trauma, unusual sleep postures, manipulation of the head and neck (as can occur in chiropractic practice), and other trivial causes such as severe coughing, nose blowing or sexual intercourse. Again, medical pathologic states including Marfan's syndrome, cystic medial degeneration, fibromuscular dysplasia, and infection may be predisposing factors.

The outcome can be complete resolution, permanent neurologic deficits, or, in 10% of patients, death. Recurrences are known to occur, and long-term anticoagulation is a controversial issue, presently recommended for up to 3 months to decrease embolic risk. Immediate therapy is also open to controversy but favors the use of heparin followed by warfarin. Thrombolytic therapy is beginning to be utilized in the early (less than 4 hours and preferably less than 2 hours) onset of acute nonhemorrhage stroke of thrombotic or embolic origin. Its use in stroke secondary to nonaortic arterial dissections is not presently defined. For aortic dissection, hemolytic agents are contraindicated, as their use can contribute to a catastrophic event. **Corticosteroid therapy** given in higher doses, such as those given to patients with rheumatoid arthritis and other inflammatory diseases, have been shown to have a relative risk of 2.73% of having a cardiovascular event when compared to a control group. These events included myocardial infarction, angina, coronary revascularization, angioplasty, heart failure, stroke, transient cerebral ischemic attack, or cardiovascular death, according to a Scottish study reported in 2003.

Any blood vessel, either artery or vein, may become subject to insult by a variety of pathogens, toxins, inflammatory or coagulopathic disease states, and external factors such as radiation-induced injury.

Thromboembolic disease such as an acute pulmonary embolism has been known to produce **acute right ventricular infarction** in patients with normal coronary arteries. Necrosis in such cases has been found to be transmural as well as subendocardial.[62] It is believed that severe right ventricular strain is the cause of the myocardial injury in these cases.

Vasculitis (inflammatory disease of a blood vessel), with or without a necrotizing accompaniment, can occur as a result of numerous extraneous factors and inherent influences. Allergic and sensitivity reactions to multiple drugs are becoming more frequent as pharmacologic therapy increases in scope and magnitude. Vasculitis is a common accompaniment of the various rheumatoid-collagen disease states.

Radiation-induced vasculitis is known to produce occlusive disease of the arterial and venous systems. It can follow radiation therapy for malignant tumors at varying locations many years after cessation of therapy, and is also known to enhance the progression of arterio-atherosclerosis in the involved arteries. Symptoms and signs vary according to the blood vessel involved (artery or vein) and the anatomic structure and location of the vessel. Thrombo-occlusive lesions may occur in any organ system or location, producing the resultant clinical pathophysiology.

Review of the medical literature is indicative that the formerly stated opinions of the heart and blood vessels being resistant to radiation are not valid. These effects, as logic would dictate, are influenced by the following logistics: location, dose-fractionation, total dose, duration of exposure, degree of shielding, and possibly the concomitant use of chemotherapy.

Thrombo-occlusive disease produced by radiation-induced vasculitis with subsequent enhanced atherosclerosis and its pathophysiologic consequences is now being seen more often in patients who received radiation therapy 20 or more years previously.

Hull et al. reported a 7.4% incidence of **carotid** and/or **subclavian artery stenosis** in survivors of Hodgkin's lymphoma treated with radiation therapy.[63] Their report also noted a 10.4% incidence of coronary artery disease and a 6.2% incidence of valvular dysfunction in a study involving 415 patients. Statistical analysis and epidemiologic comparison revealed that these were statistically higher rates than would be expected in the general population.

Pericardial disease is the commonest manifestation of **radiation-induced cardiac injury. The resultant pericarditis** can be acute, subacute, or chronic, with all the typical signs, symptoms, and sequelae of other forms of pericarditis including those of effusion, hemopericardium, and constriction.

It has become increasingly apparent that radiation therapy to the mediastinum can injure all cardiac structures. **Aortic stenosis and insufficiency, mitral insufficiency, tricuspid insufficiency**, and **occlusive coronary artery disease** are all known to occur following mediastinal radiation. A retrospective study of 294 patients by way of history, physical examination, electrocardiograph, and echocardiographic interrogation, found a high prevalence of asymptomatic heart disease in this patient population in general, particularly that of aortic valvular disease.[64]

This study revealed an increased prevalence of electrocardiographic left ventricular hypertrophy, right bundle branch block, abnormal Q-waves, and high resting heart rate. In addition to the increased incidence of pericardial thickening (21%), the researchers noted previously unreported findings of a progressive decrease in left ventricular mass, diastolic cavity dimensions, and wall thickness, indicative of **radiation-induced cardiomyopathic atrophy and fibrosis.** Editorial commentary accompanying the review noted that subcarinal blocking techniques to limit radiation-induced heart disease did not significantly reduce the risk of myocardial infarction, but did reduce the incidence of other forms of cardiac injury.[65] They further noted that the risk of radiation-induced heart disease may be increased by the concomitant use of anthracycline-based chemotherapy, as when larger doses of doxorubicin are given. Whether or not these studies are as applicable to other pathologic conditions for which thoracic radiation is utilized is at present uncertain.

Cayenne et al. reported a case of documented left main and right **coronary ostial stenosis** in a 44-year-old female who received thoracic radiation for Hodgkin's disease of more than 20 years status.

Bilateral internal carotid artery disease with total occlusion of the right internal carotid artery and subcritical occlusion of the left internal carotid artery was reported in a patient suffering from transient cerebral ischemic attacks who had been treated with cervical radiation for squamous call carcinoma of the pharynx 5 years previously.[67]

Yokoi et al.[68] reported **Takayasu's arteritis** associated with positive tests for lupus anticoagulant and elevated anticardiolipin antibody titers in two patients. This was an unusual association because vasculitis was observed in a patient that involved the smaller arteries. This form of idiopathic (possibly an immunogenic-induced phenomenon to an as yet unknown inciting factor) vasculitis generally involves the larger arteries: the aorta and all its branches, pulmonary arteries, and renal arteries. It is more common in young females of Asian extraction and can result in heart failure, hypertension, stroke symptoms, renal failure, and various other organ symptomatology. Its treatment is similar to that of giant cell arteritis, that is, corticosteroids and anti-immunologic agents.

Setoguchi et al.[69] reported **aorto-iliac occlusive disease** associated with lupus anticoagulant in two young males. This was an uncommon situation because both patients were young men without evidence of other risk factors for the development of atherosclerotic occlusion. Furthermore, thromboembolic episodes associated with this immunoglobulin usually involve the smaller-sized arteries or veins.

Vasculitis can be an accompaniment of any **collagen or rheumatoid disease** state and presents in many guises. An uncommon case of superior vena cava syndrome secondary to **Behcet's disease** was reported in a 29-year-old male.[70] Behcet's disease is an often-overlooked chronic multisystem disease classified with other more common autoimmune vasculopathies: systemic lupus erythematosus, polyarteritis, polyarteritis nodosa, scleroderma, dermatomyositis, polymyositis, mixed collagen disease, and so on. It usually presents with oral, genital, ocular, and dermatalogic manifestations and can involve any artery or vein, producing occlusive vasculitis. Bardakci et al. reported an unusual and uncommon presentation of **Behcet's syndrome** in a 25-year-old male, which required surgery for an aortic arch aneurysm with pseudocoarctation, and a markedly occluded proximal left anterior descending coronary artery caused by vasculitis. The vasculitis in Behcet's syndrome can involve the venous and arterial systems.

Temporal arteritis (giant cell arteritis) is an inflammatory vasculitis of unknown etiology affecting larger arteries. It is a commonly overlooked and misdiagnosed entity usually affecting women over 50 years of age, but may affect any gender at any age. It is accompanied by an elevated erythrocyte sedimentation rate, mild anemia, and sometimes leukocytosis and hypergammaglobulinemia. The diagnosis is usually confirmed by unilateral or bilateral temporal artery biopsy, which reveals lymphocyte infiltration, giant cells, and disruption of the elastic lamina. Its most feared and frequent complication is unilateral or bilateral blindness caused by retinal artery occlusion and ischemic optic neuropathy. A high degree of suspicion must be exercised, as even patients who present with nontender, nonswollen temporal arteries may be affected. Initial symptoms can be misleading and can occur in many less-involved conditions and include headache, jaw pain, varying degrees and types of visual disturbances, and vague systemic symptoms. Further leading one away from the accurate diagnosis is the not infrequent accompaniment of **polymyalgia rheumatica**, also associated with a high sedimentation rate and various systemic and nonspecific symptoms.

Traumatic veno-occlusive disease of the upper and lower extremities can occur after numerous types of physical, exertional, or iatrogenic trauma. Upper and lower extremity venous thrombosis can produce pulmonary embolism. If not diagnosed and treated promptly, chronic post-thrombotic syndrome may occur and lead to extremity-disabling symptoms and problems. Diagnostic procedures include duplex venous ultrasonography, MRI, and venography. Therapy includes thrombolysis, anticoagulation, and surgery. Goel et al. reported a typical case of effort-related subclavian vein thrombosis and its successful management.

Coagulopathic Disorders

9

Basic Coagulation Defects

Increasing attention is being given to inherited abnormalities of the body's anticoagulation system: deficiencies of antithrombin III, protein C and protein S, and the increased prothrombotic state caused by a genetic defect (mutation) of factor V Leiden causing activated protein C resistance. Proper functioning of these systems is necessary to prevent arterial and venous thrombo-occlusive disease, predominantly the latter. In these cases, especially those with arterial involvement, the search for hyperhomocysteinemia and the presence of antiphospholipid antibodies is also in order.

Any individual with a positive coagulopathic or thrombotic state, and those with otherwise inexplicable thrombo-embolic episodes, especially if recurrent, should be adequately investigated for the possible presence of a hypercoagulable state. This would include an appropricate assay of **protein C and S, antithrombin III** and the **anti-phospholipid antibody syndrome**, which includes lupus anticoagulant and anticardiolipin antibodies.

Factor V Leiden mutation can be present in 3 to 7% of the population, whereas the prothrombin mutation occurs in 1 to 4% of the population. With appropriate laboratory testing, it is now possible to identify a predisposing genetic cause in approximately 50% of patients who have had one or more venous thromboembolic events. **Protein C deficiency** is said to occur in 1:200 to 1:300 persons in the general population, and **protein S deficiency** may be just as common. Proteins C and S are vitamin K dependent and inhibit factors V and VIII. Antithrombin III prevents the continued action of thrombin and factors IX and X. **Heparin** causes antithrombin III to become an instantaneous inhibitor of the coagulation enzymes thrombin, factors IX, and X.

In patients predisposed to a hypercoagulable state, it must be remembered that warfarin may decrease the levels of protein C and S, which can result in a dangerous paradoxical response by causing hyperactivation of the clotting mechanism. It can also predispose one to **warfarin-induced skin necrosis**. Numerous factors can alter the state of, and interfere with, the assays of the various anticoagulation factors. As stated, warfarin decreases the levels of protein C and S. Heparin causes a decrease in plasma antithrombin activity, and acute thrombosis can decrease antithrombin III and protein C and S. The more common factors that predispose to hypercoagulability of the blood are listed in Table 9.1.

Table 9.1 Factors Predisposing to Hypercoagulability

Inherited anticoagulation deficiencies
Immobility
Trauma
Pregnancy
Postoperative state
Cancer
Contraceptives
Heart failure
Infection (disseminated intravascular coagulation)
Heparin-induced thrombocytopenia
Homocysteinemia
Idiopathic and secondary forms of antiphospholipid syndrome
Liver disease
Renal failure

Primary antiphospholipid syndrome is uncommon compared to the usual secondary causes. The commonest inciting factors that predispose one to the development of antiphospholipid syndrome are the collagen and rheumatoid diseases, especially lupus erythematosus, viral infections, and lymphoma. Drugs such as procainamide and apresoline are also known to produce a lupus-like syndrome with or without the presence of antiphospholipid syndrome. The risk of venous thrombosis in the female population taking oral contraceptives is three to five times greater than in nonusers, but in those with factor V Leiden deficiencies it can be quadrupled beyond that level, and is known to increase the risk of venous thrombosis in these women by as much as 35-fold.[71]

The presence of heterozygous **factor V Leiden mutation** is said to occur in up to 5.2% of the white American population, and decreases to about less than one-half to one-fourth of that level in other ethnic groups,[72] whereas 2% are heterozygous for the **prothrombin G20210A mutation**. Individuals so afflicted have been shown to have a sevenfold increased risk of venous thromboembolism.[72] The increased risk of deep venous thrombosis associated with hypercoagulable states occurs with greatest frequency in the lower extremities. Martinelli et al. found a prevalence of hypercoagulable states in 15% of patients with thrombosis of the upper extremities, compared to 56% of those with lower extremity thrombosis. They concluded that the presence of a hypercoagulable state is low in patients with primary deep vein thrombosis of the arms and that the usual inciting factor was strenuous exercise of the muscles in the affected extremity.[73]

A patient with mural thrombosis of the thoracic aorta and thromboembolism to the mesenteric artery has been reported in association with protein C and S deficiency.[74]

Cerebral, inferior vena caval and iliofemoral venous thrombosis were reported in a young female who began oral contraceptives 10 days previously and was subsequently found to have combined **protein C deficiency** and **activated protein C resistance**. The patient was successfully treated with heparin and later continued on warfarin.[75]

Although debate continues as to whether or not all women who are planning to **use contraceptives** should be checked for activated protein C resistance, there is much less debate that any young female who develops her first bout of venous thrombosis (especially if taking contraceptives) should be investigated for a hypercoagulable state, mainly that of activated protein C resistance. Some investigators also believe that in male patients, a similar plan should be followed, especially if no inciting extraneous cause is discovered.

Glueck et al. have recommended that all women who are on or plan to begin estrogen replacement therapy be checked to detect those who are heterozygous for factor V Leiden mutation (4%). These patients would have a relative or absolute contraindication to estrogen therapy because of their markedly increased risk of atherothrombosis and thromboembolism.[76]

It is of interest that Glueck et al. previously recommended that before placing women on estrogen therapy, plasma triglyceride levels be measured because of the marked hypertriglyceridemia that can occur following their use, thereby avoiding the increased incidence of associated pancreatitis, myocardial infarction, and stroke.

Bilateral thalamic infarction in a 50-year-old man who had no other risk factors for causation of stroke other than heterozygous factor V Leiden mutation was reported.[77] Extensive clinical and laboratory evaluation did not reveal any possible origin of thromboembolism. The patient was treated with warfarin with partial resolution of the neurologic abnormalities. The authors of the report also indicated that children with heterozygous **activated protein C resistance (APCR)** are at increased risk for stroke. The overall risk for venous thromboembolism in people with APCR has been calculated as 3-fold for heterozygotes and 18-fold for homozygotes compared to noncarriers.[78] Particular attention must be given to pregnant patients, as pregnancy itself is a significant risk factor for the development of thromboembolism. When pregnancy occurs in the presence of any coagulopathy, the results can be catastrophic. Approximately 60% of women who develop venous thrombosis during pregnancy are positive for APCR. This can be easily evaluated by performing a DNA-based assay for factor V abnormality. This is in contrast to those with protein C deficiency, which occurs in 5 to 7% of young nonpregnant women with venous thromboembolism, 6 to 8% with protein S deficiency and 2% with antithrombin III deficiency. In nonpregnant women with a history of venous thromboembolism, APCR is said to occur in 30 to 40% of patients.

Management of the pregnant patient diagnosed with venous thrombosis or thromboembolism can be taxing. Prompt evaluation for coagulopathic disorders must be done and urgent treatment initiated. Warfarin, of course, should not be used during pregnancy because it crosses the placental barrier and increases the risk of fetal hemorrhage, birth defects, and miscarriage. Heparin is the drug of choice in the pregnant patient. Aspirin is of no value in activated protein C resistance (APCR) but can be utilized in cases of anticardiolipin syndrome. The convenience with which low-molecular-weight heparin can be utilized has made it the drug of choice in the pregnant, as well as the nonpregnant, patient.

Patients who are diagnosed as having the **antiphospholipid syndrome** (APLS) are initially managed with heparin during an acute event, followed by warfarin and aspirin (the latter if arterial embolism has occurred). A decision must then be made about the duration of anticoagulation in which oral anticoagulants are generally given, often for an indefinite period of time.[79] Although prolonged anticoagulation is the treatment of choice for patients who have sustained a thrombotic event associated with APLS, it has been shown that recurrence during anticoagulation was high and usually occurred in the same territory as the original thrombosis.[80]

APLS patients may suffer complications beyond the well-known realm of arterial and venous thrombosis and recurrent fetal loss. It is now realized that this condition may be complicated by cardiac valvular disease, livedo reticularis, and thrombocytopenia. The management of these patients during the perioperative period (especially during contemplated cardiac valvular surgery) is exceptionally complex in terms of therapy and laboratory testing.[81]

Thromboembolic pulmonary embolism, producing pulmonary hypertension and acute respiratory distress syndrome (ARDS), have been associated with APLS secondary to systemic lupus and Sjogren's syndrome. In addition, a fatal noninflammatory pulmonary vasculopathy may occur, with its fulminant progress being nonresponsive to all known medical measures.[82] Finally, much controversy still exists about what is the best course for long-term management of patients with APLS who have suffered a thromboembolic event, as monitoring these patients when on warfarin and utilizing standard prothrombin time and INR determinations may be inadequate.[83]

In the past, APLS was generally thought to be associated with systemic lupus erythematosus and other collagen diseases, but it is now classified as a predominantly independent autoimmune disorder. Initial thrombotic events are presently treated with heparin, and in cases of peripheral vascular disease and pregnancy, outcomes have been shown to be improved by the addition of aspirin when feasible.[84] Therefore, even though underlying disease states should be considered in a differential diagnosis, its independence should not be forgotten. Tables 9.2 and 9.3 review the clinical features and thrombotic complications of APLS.

Whenever APLS is suspected, antiphospholipid antibodies should be determined, including anticardiolipin antibodies and lupus anticoagulant. Antiphospholipid antibodies may be seen in up to 40% of patients with

Table 9.2 Features that are Associated with APS but are not Criteria

Clinical[a]	Laboratory
Livedo reticularis Thrombocytopenia Hemolytic anemia Transverse myelopathy Transient cerebral ischemia Amaurosis fugax Cardiac valvulopathy Seizures Chorea Hemiballismus	Antibodies to Beta2, GPI Negatively charged phospholipids (e.g., phosphatidylserine, phosphatidylinositol, phosphatidylglycerol, phosphatidic acid) Neutral phospholipids (e.g., phosphatidylethanolamine, phosphatidylserine) Prothrombin, protein C, protein S, C4b-binding protein Annexins Low-positive aCL antibody test results Positive IgA aCL antibody test results False-positive syphilis (treponemal) test results

Source: From Wilson, W.A., Crump, J. W., J. *Musculoskel. Med.*, 22:9–20, 2005. With permission.
Note: APS, antiphospholipid syndrome; Beta2 GPI, Beta2-glycoprotein-l; aCL, anticardiolipin.
[a] If thrombosis is demonstrated by imaging or biopsy, clinical criteria for thrombosis are met.

Table 9.3 Clinical Presentations of Thrombosis in APS

System	Presentation
Cardiac	Angina, myocardial infarction, cardiac valve disease with thromboembolization to peripheral arteries
CNS	Stroke, ischemic optic neuropathy, migraine, multiinfarct dementia, cerebral venous sinus thrombosis, chorea, hemiballismus
Cutaneous	Livedo reticularis, ulceration
GI	Thrombosis of hepatic, portal mesenteric vessels, Budd-Chiari syndrome
Hematologic	Thrombocytopenia, hemolytic anemia, thrombotic thrombocytopenic purpura
Pulmonary	Emboli, hypertension, hemorrhage
Renal	Renal artery stenosis, renal vein thrombosis, renal infarction, proteinuria, renal failure

Source: From Wilson, W. A., Crump, J. W., *J. Musculoskel. Med.*, 22:9–20, 2005. With permission.
Note: APS, antiphospholipid syndrome.

systemic lupus erythematosis, and approximately one-third of these patients develop APLS. More recently, cognitive deficits were shown to be present in 42% of patients diagnosed with APLS.[85]

It may be necessary to investigate the so-called idiopathic thromboembolic states for the previously noted coagulopathic conditions, but patients with a history of arterial or venous thrombosis, including the microvasculature, should be investigated for APLS. This includes those patients who have had a history of fetal loss and premature births. Basic tests should include an evaluation for the presence of anticardiolipin antibodies and lupus anticoagulant and if need be, repeating both 6 weeks later. If the results are negative or inconclusive, and the diagnosis appears to be firmly established clinically, more esoteric studies can be contemplated.[84] Tables 9.2 and 9.3 summarize the clinical and organ-specific features and presentations.

Von Willebrand disease (vWD) is a hereditable autosomal dominant hemorrhagic disorder that affects 1 to 3% of the population, involving both sexes, and is due to a structural or functional deficiency of the von Willebrand protein factor (vWF). It is classified into three subtypes and is often unrecognized until precipitated by trauma or surgery. It is manifest as easy bruising and bleeding that can be exacerbated by aspirin and other nonsteroidal anti-inflammatory drugs (NSAIDs). The predominant manifestations are those associated with hemorrhage (Table 9.4).

Acquired **von Willebrand disease** (AvWD) is usually found in elderly patients in association with numerous disease states[86] (Table 9.5).

Table 9.4 Clinical Manifestations of von Willebrand Disease (vWD)

Bruising
Bleeding
Mucosal hemorrhage
Menorrhagia
Subcutaneous hemorrhage
Intramuscular hemorrhage
Hemarthroses
Intracranial hemorrhage

Table 9.5 Disease States and Other Factors Associated with Acquired von Willebrand Disease

Lymphoproliferative disorders
Chronic lymphocytic leukemia
Hairy cell leukemia
Non-Hodgkin lymphoma
Plasma cell proliferative disorders
MGUS
Waldenstrom macroglobulinemia
Multiple myeloma
Myeloproliferative disorders
Chronic myeloid leukemia
Essential thrombocythemia
Polycythemia vera

(Continued)

Table 9.5 (Continued)

Neoplasmic disorders
Wilms tumor
Adrenocortical carcinoma
Lung cancer
Peripheral neuroectodermal tumor
Gastric carcinoma
Acute lymphoblastic leukemia
Autoimmune states
Systemic lupus erythematosus
Scleroderma
Mixed connective tissue disease
Felty syndrome
Autoimmune hemolytic anemia
Endocrine disorders
Hypothyroidism
Diabetes mellitus
Drugs
Ciprofloxacin
Valproic acid
Hydroxyethyl starch
Recombinant factor VIII infusion
Griseofulvin
Others
Embryonal adenoma of kidney
Amyloidosis
Angiodysplasia
Hemoglobin E beta-thalassemia
Ehlers-Danlos syndrome
Excessive fibrinolysis
Epstein-Barr virus infection
Allogeneic bone marrow transplant
Hydatid disease
Pesticide ingestion
Reactive thrombocytosis
Glycogen storage disease
Uremia
Mitral valve prolapse
Congenital heart disease

Source: From Kumar, S., Pruthi, R.K., Nichols, W.L., *Mayo Clin. Proc.* 77:181–187, 2002. With permission.

Note: MGUS, monoclonal gammopathy of undertmined significance.

The von Willebrand abnormality is considered to be a rare and often overlooked entity. Coagulation screening tests may vary in degrees of abnormality and may even be normal, including the simple bleeding time, prothrombin time, partial thromboplastin time, and factor VIII activity, necessitating specific tests of vWF antigen and ristocetin cofactor activity. Conversion of the more debilitating type 2vWBd to the less involved type I following aortic valve replacement has been reported.[87] Patients with aortic stenosis and insufficiency as well as mitral stenosis with regurgitation are known to acquire a bleeding disorder or coagulopathy that resembles vWBd, which is either partially corrected or normalized by appropriate valvular surgery. Interestingly, acute myocardial infarction can rarely occur in vWd patients.[88] It becomes a therapeutic dilemma, but percutaneous intervention with carefully monitored anticoagulation therapy has been successful.[88] Equally complicated is the coexistence of factor V Leiden and primary antiphospholipid–syndrome-causing recurrent myocardial infarction in a patient with thrombocytopenia. This suggests that under questionable and appropriate circumstances, a multifaceted diagnostic approach may be required to arrive at an appropriate diagnosis and therapeutic decision.[89]

Heparin-Induced Thrombocytopenia

Heparin-induced thrombocytopenia (HIT) is becoming more prevalent due to the advent of increasing use of anticoagulation for the treatment and prophylaxis of various thromboembolic disorders. Often overlooked, it is also being widely recognized by attending and consulting physicians. It can be a potentially catastrophic event when overlooked. It is triggered by exposure to heparin therapy, usually unfractionated heparin, even in the smallest amounts, as associated with intravenous flushes or short-term therapeutic or prophylactic doses. It should be strongly considered in the event of platelet counts decreasing to levels of 100 to 150,000 from previously normal levels, especially when associated with an unexpected thromboembolic event, which occurs in 50 to 66% of patients, with an accompanying mortality as high as 30%.[90] The overall incidence of HIT has been reported as less than 1% and varying from 2 to 4%. A decrease in the platelet count of 50% or greater, regardless of the original level, should cause immediate suspicion of the presence of HIT.

Additional clues are the presence of thrombosis (venous or arterial) and bleeding (external or internal). A history of heparin exposure should be sought—even the use of guide wires and catheters coated with heparin, prosthetic devices, and minimal heparin flushes. HIT is an immune-complex reaction composed of IgG binding to heparin and platelet factor 4 that triggers the activation of platelets and endothelial factors, causing the release of procoagulant particles that initiate thrombin generation and endothelial injury.[91] Most cases occur in surgical patients but can follow even the most innocent noninvasive procedures. HIT can be divided into types 1 and 2. Type 1 is the innocent occurrence of a decreased platelet count that occurs in 10 to 20% of patients within 4 days of receiving heparin and is generally reversible even on continuing heparin.

Type 2 occurs on exposure to heparin usually after 5 to 14 days, is not reversible on discontinuing heparin, and leads to complications of thromboembolism in up to 50% of patients, with a mortality of 50% or higher. It can occur in 10 hours or less in patients who have previously been exposed to heparin. The complications can be numerous and devastating (Table 9.6). HIT may also be delayed in occurrence for periods of time greater than 2 weeks, with thrombosis rates as high as 51% at 30 days.[90,92]

The diagnosis first requires suspicion, and can be assisted in its confirmation or refutation by laboratory assays for antiplatelet antibodies (PF4). Tests currently used vary in sensitivity and specificity. Most patients with HIT have a positive test, which can also occur in patients who do not have HIT.

Table 9.6 Thrombotic and Other Sequelae of HIT

Venous thrombosis

- Deep venous thrombosis (DVT)
- Warfarin-induced venous limb gangrene
- Pulmonary embolism
- Cerebral vein (dural sinus) thrombosis
- Adrenal hemorrhagic infarction

Arterial thrombosis

- Aortic or iliofemoral thrombosis resulting in acute limb ischemia or infarction
- Acute thrombotic stroke
- Myocardial infarction
- Cardiac intraventricular or intra-atrial thrombosis in situ or via embolization of DVT
- Thrombosis involving miscellaneous arteries
- Embolization of thrombus from heart or proximal aorta can also contribute to microvascular ischemic syndrome
- Microvascular thrombosis

Miscellaneous

- Heparin-induced skin lesions at heparin injection site
- Coumarin-induced skin necrosis complicating HIT involving central sites
- Acute systemic reactions after IV heparin bolus
- Disseminated intravascular coagulation with hypofibrinogenemia and acquired natural anticoagulant deficiency

Source: From *CME Today*. May, 2003. Medical Education Broadcast Network. With permission.

The platelet antibody assay by ELISA is more often positive in coagulopathic disorders that are not due to HIT, and the serotonin release assay (SRA) is more specific for HIT.[93] None are diagnostic. Sensitivity and specificity for the platelet injury assay by serotonin release are stated as being 88 and 100%, respectively, whereas that of the platelet aggregation assay is stated as being 91 and 77%, and the most frequently performed ELISA antibody test as 90 to 97% and 86%.[94,95] The ELISA test measures only the presence of antibodies and is not diagnostic of HIT, so when positive, it must be combined with an activation and antigen assay as noted above. The general consensus in evaluating the three usual laboratory tests for HIT is that if two tests are negative (i.e., ELISA and SRA), HIT is not present. If both are positive, the presence of HIT is confirmed.

During a question and answer period following his lecture on HIT (September, 2007), Dr. Warkentin one of the world's foremost researchers on HIT, responded:

Q: It is often stated that no tests are diagnostic of HIT. What is your opinion?
A: I disagree. If the SRA is positive, the patient has HIT.
Q: It has been reported that HIT can begin 30 or more days after discontinuing heparin.
A: I disagree. This is usually not the case. One must check the timing, clinical and laboratory parameters and rule out pseudo-HIT or earlier HIT in progress.
Q: What should be done if a patient has a combination of HIT and disseminated intravascular coagulation (DIC)?
A: Treat the HIT and allow the DIC to manage itself (dependent upon the underlying pathology).
Q: If a patient had a history of HIT 6 years previously and anticoagulation is necessary, can heparin be given?
A: Yes, as there is no "immune memory" to HIT pathophysiology.

Dr. Warkentin also noted that quinine, vancomycin, and antiplatelet agents of the glycoprotein IIB and IIIA inhibitor class and the thienopyridines can cause severe thrombocytopenia and are erroneously diagnosed as HIT in some patients.

Therapy involves the immediate cessation of heparin and administration of a direct thrombin inhibitor (DTI) for type 2 HIT. Some specialists treating this disorder are proponents of administration of thrombin inhibitors in patients with type 1 HIT to prevent the initiation and progression of thrombosis. In severe cases additional therapy with antiplatelet agents and intravenous immune globulin may be necessary.

The direct thrombin inhibitors approved for use are lepirudin and argatroban. Lepirudin is cleared by the kidneys and must be used with caution under the circumstance of renal insufficiency and elevated serum creatinine. Argatroban can be used in these cases, but must be avoided in patients with hepatic disease or dysfunction, in which case lepirudin can be used.

What To Do When HIT is Suspected[96,97]

Stop heparin immediately.

DO NOT begin anticoagulation with warfarin.

DO NOT change to low-molecular-weight heparin.

Assess clinical status and obtain appropriate laboratory studies.

DO NOT rely solely on a normal platelet count.

If necessary, rule out other causes of thrombocytopenia and bleeding.

DO NOT rely solely on antibody testing to make a diagnosis.

If a patient has been treated with heparin during the previous 6 months or was known to have reactive thrombocytopenia, obtain platelet counts every day when reinstituting therapy. Continue for 4 to 5 days and then every second or third day, according to status and individual judgment.

Remember that HIT is more common than diagnosed or suspected.

Remember that HIT type 2 can presumably occur several weeks after previous treatment with heparin, so one must consider making a delayed diagnosis.

DO NOT wait for results of tests when HIT is considered as a plausible diagnosis. Begin DTI (direct thrombin inhibitor) treatment, and then assess the patient, results of tests, and pre- and post-test probability of the disease being present.

DO NOT begin warfarin until the patient is adequately anticoagulated with a DTI.

Use full doses of DTIs.

Obtain cardiac and/or hematologic consultation.

The use of low-molecular-weight heparin is considerably less productive in the causation of HIT, except in patients who already have had the diagnosis.

Patients previously receiving heparin for 3 months or less, and undergoing cardiovascular interventions during which heparin may be utilized should undergo HIT antibody testing.

Patients with a history of HIT, regardless of the time period, should undergo HIT antibody testing and preferably be given a DTI, even in the face of a negative antibody study.

Limiting the use of heparin or low-molecular-weight heparin to a period of 5 days or less can minimize the production of HIT.

Platelet transfusions are contraindicated in the treatment of HIT.

Cancer patients have a greater increased risk for the development of venous thrombosis, especially within the first year of diagnosis and if metastases are present. Those with additional and usually undiagnosed coagulopathic disorders (e.g., factor V Leiden, prothrombin mutations, etc.) have a much higher risk.[98]

A presentation by D. Kress at the 2005 annual meeting of the American College of Chest Physicians in Montreal reported an increase in postoperative cardiac surgery complications in patients without evidence of HIT but with HPF-4 antibodies on preoperative laboratory screening.

Additional Coagulation Commentary

Prothrombin, protein C, and protein S are vitamin K dependent. Antithrombin III prevents the continued action of thrombin and factors IX and X. In the usually performed assays of all three factors (C, S, AT III), only 25% of patients with inherent coagulation disorders are diagnosed. All three prevent continued blood coagulation. Heparin causes AT III to become an instantaneous inhibitor of the coagulation enzymes, including thrombin and factors IX and X. Protein C and S inhibit factors V and VIII and are measured by immunoassay of the plasma antigen level. When assessing antithrombin III levels, it is important to request the AT III concentration by immunoassay and the plasma antithrombin and heparin cofactor activity with functional assays. Protein C– and S–deficient heterozygotes have 50% of the normal range for these factors and are at an increased risk for thrombosis. Administration of heparin decreases plasma antithrombin activity, and warfarin decreases the level of proteins C and S. Therefore, it is imperative when using warfarin that one observe patients for a dangerous paradoxical response that enhances clotting and predisposes the patient to warfarin-induced skin necrosis.

Disseminated intravascular coagulation syndrome is often confused with HIT 2 because of the associated thrombocytopenia. It can occur in numerous pathophysiologic abnormalities and is important to recognize, because its management is the opposite of that utilized for HIT (Table 9.7).

In addition to a decreased platelet count, there is an increase in the prothrombin time and partial thromboplastin time and increased fibrin degradation products as found with an elevated D-dimer assay. Fibrinogen levels are decreased in severe cases, which can be alleviated by the administration of plasma cryoprecipitate, which is fibrinogen enriched. DIC is noted to produce severe hemorrhagic episodes in various organs and anatomic locations, in contrast to the mainly thromboembolic events caused by HIT. When DIC is suspected, one should also check for the presence of AT III and protein C

Table 9.7 Causes of Disseminated Intravascular Coagulation

Causes
Infection
Surgical and obstetrical procedures and complications
Malignant neoplasms
Severe liver and pancreatic disease
Snake bites

and S deficiencies as well as for the presence of antiphospholipid antibodies (lupus anticoagulant and anticardiolipin antibodies). DIC is managed by correction of the inducing pathologic states, platelet transfusion, plasma cryoprecipitate (fresh frozen plasma), low-dose heparin, and epsilon aminocaproic acid when blood components fail to control hemorrhage. Antithrombin III administration may sometimes be of value.

Mesenteric Ischemia

10

Mesenteric ischemia may be acute and instantaneous or chronically progressive. The diagnosis of either form can be very difficult, seemingly enigmatic, and quite often overlooked until surgery or death occurs. It can be classified as one of the most difficult diagnoses to make and is often a considerable medical and surgical management problem as well. The symptoms and diagnostic signs or clues may be nonspecific, all of which too often lead to delayed diagnosis, high morbidity, and a substantial increase in mortality. Bowel necrosis (gangrene of the bowel) begins as early as a few hours (up to 12 hours), with a mortality of 80%, depending on the extent and distribution of the arterial occlusion. The acute form is generally thromboembolic, more often embolic, and less so, inherently thrombotic. The underlying substrate is usually a patient with comorbid conditions such as coronary heart disease with previous myocardial infarction, valvular heart disease, atrial fibrillation, heart failure, aortic atherosclerosis, or mesenteric atherosclerosis. A rare case of acute mesenteric ischemia causing thrombosis of the celiac and superior mesenteric arteries due to **activated protein C resistance** was reported by Scally et al.

The acute form can be quite sudden and is known to mimic almost any acute abdominal condition. These include diseases of the gallbladder, pancreas, other intestinal pathologies; perforated viscus, diverticulitis with rupture, appendicitis with rupture, and any condition productive of peritonitis. The diagnosis requires a combination of suspicion, diligence, and clinical acumen. Once gangrenous necrosis begins and peritonitis occurs, a mortality as high as 90% can be expected, death being due to multiorgan failure, often with sepsis. A major clue pointing to the diagnosis is unremitting abdominal pain that is generally diffuse and nonlocalized, at times associated with nausea, vomiting, diarrhea, and, rarely, bloody stool. It is usually unrelieved by intravenous narcotics. The pathophysiology has been well-described by Oldenburg et al., who noted that the splanchnic circulation receives 25% of the resting cardiac output and up to 35% of the postprandial cardiac output.[99]

It is the delay in contemplating the diagnosis that leads to the delay in performing appropriate diagnostic studies, thus delaying the available therapeutic measures and resulting in the high mortality. Pre-interventional administration of intra-arterial papaverine and intravenous dobutamine may be of value in some cases and may protect tissue as well as reperfusion injury prior to endovascular stenting, surgical vascular repair, or bowel resection.[100]

The chronic form of mesenteric ischemia is often less demanding of thought and action. It usually occurs in patients who have a history of atherosclerotic vascular disease and present with intermittent or progressive abdominal symptoms, frequently described as abdominal angina, which produces postprandial abdominal cramps or pain. Nonocclusive mesenteric ischemia can be equally as fatal because it generally occurs in very ill patients who are hemodynamically stressed and are compromised by decreased visceral perfusion superimposed upon diffuse atherosclerosis.[100]

Mesenteric venous ischemia may also present with vague or diffuse abdominal pain over a few days, accompanied by fear of eating, diarrhea, bloody stools, hemorrhagic ascites, fever, and hypotensive dehydration. It is generally associated with various risk factors such as hypercoagulable states, surgical procedures, cancer, abdominal inflammatory disorders, and venous stasis, as can be seen in patients with cirrhosis and portal hypertension.[100] In mesenteric venous occlusive states, rapid initiation of a CT angiogram and infusion with intravenous heparin can decrease the morbidity and subsequent mortality. Diagnostic measures utilized are abdominal ultrasound, CT angiography, MR angiography and direct angiography.

The applicable invasive procedures for acute and chronic mesenteric ischemia include direct surgical revascularization, angioplasty with stent placement, and bowel resection. Bowel resection is usually necessary if the ischemic gangrenous window of 8 hours is exceeded.[101,102] Acute arterial occlusive mesenteric ischemia has been reported to occur in 80% of cases, with 65% of those being embolic or thrombotic.[102] The remaining 20% of cases with mesenteric arterial ischemia are of the chronic variety, allowing more time for clinical evaluation, diagnostic studies, and treatment. A prompt diagnosis followed by immediate therapy is required if the high degree of mortality is to be reduced, which is as great as 90% once a severe state of ischemic gangrene with peritonitis occurs. This is accompanied by dehydration, lactic acidosis, sepsis, shock, and multiorgan failure.

Venous mesenteric ischemia generally allows the attending physician or consultant more time for evaluation. Early diagnosis is preferable so that intravenous heparin can be given. The use of thrombolytic therapy for acute arterial mesenteric ischemia is under investigation.

Specific Cardiopathic Disorders

IV

11 Pericardial Problems

The pericardium can be the source of numerous primary and secondary diseases. The double sac (parietal and visceral) fibrous structure is normally separated by 15 to 50 cc of plasma-derived fluid. It serves important anatomic and physiologic functions, even though it is not necessary for survival. The commonest pathologic abnormality affecting the pericardium is acute pericarditis. The commonest cause of pericarditis, in general, is idiopathic acute pericarditis, usually of viral etiology. The inflammation may be fibrinous, effusive, or hemorrhagic. Pericardial involvement due to blunt chest trauma is often overlooked. Partial absence of the pericardium (congenital pericardial defects) have been known to cause cardiac and vascular herniation, strangulation of the left atrium, and sudden death. The pericardium serves as a communicative crossroad for pathology produced by many diseases. These include viral, bacterial, and protozoal pathogens; numerous drugs; primary and secondary neoplasms; chemical toxins; metabolic diseases; rheumatoid (collagen) vascular diseases; radiation; and secondary immune states (post–myocardial infarction syndrome, postpericardiotomy syndrome).

The commonest side effect of pericardial pathology is pericardial effusion. The effusion can be serous, hemorrhagic, empyemic, or any combination of these. Pericardial constriction (constrictive pericarditis) may occur over a more prolonged period of time and necessitates surgical intervention to achieve alleviation of the pathophysiologic dysfunction. Forensic medical specialists are often called to testify in cases of pericardial effusion causing pericardial tamponade, which can lead to death if not recognized and treated in time. A clinical diagnosis should be suspected in the presence of clinical symptoms (chest pain, dyspnea, tachycardia) in a patient with neck vein distension, hypotension, progressive cardiomegaly (not always present), pulsus paradoxus, and a prominent x descent and absent y descent in the jugular venous pulse. Other observations that may be of value are low voltage and electrical alternans on the ECG, the latter involving the P-QRS and T segments. Tamponade can occur with as little as 200 cc of acute accumulation of fluid or as much as 2,000 cc in slowly occurring chronic effusions. The paradoxical pulse is defined as a greater than 10-mm decrease in systolic blood pressure on inspiration. Kussmaul's sign, an increase in the jugular venous pulse on inspiration, is absent in tamponade and present in constrictive pericarditis.

The ECG in pericarditis involves four stages: acute, subacute, chronic, and recovery. The basic hallmark is a pattern of diffusely elevated ST segments with an upward concavity, appearing in the majority of limb and precordial leads. Depression of the PR segment, reflecting atrial involvement, may also be noted. After several days, the elevated ST segments progressively decline and eventually reach baseline, followed by the third stage, that of T-wave flattening and inversion. The duration of the chronic phase may be weeks or months, and is known to occur indefinitely in rare circumstances.

If the electrical alternans is significant, one may be able to palpate an alternating pulse in the peripheral arteries (pulsus alternans).

Symptomatic pericardial tamponade is a medical emergency and requires immediate intervention to avoid the physiologic "point of no return" that the patient will not survive. This can occur over a period of time varying from less than 1 hour to a few hours in some cases.

A prompt and accurate diagnosis can be made by echocardiography demonstrating the effusion and often the presence of a reduced right ventricular cavity diameter and late diastolic inward motion of the right ventricular and atrial wall (diastolic collapse). Medical therapy is of little or no value, but intravenous saline is usually administered as the patient is being readied for the necessary pericardiocentesis, along with placement of the drainage catheter or performance of a thoracotomy for making a "pericardial window" to enhance drainage and prevent recurrent tamponade. Percutaneous pericardiocentesis performed without echocardiographic guidance has a complication rate as high as 20% including heart, lung, and liver perforation; coronary artery laceration, and death.[103,104] These complications have almost been eliminated by the use of echocardiographic guidance.

An excellent overview of pericardial tamponade and large pericardial effusions presented by Kabukcu et al. found that diagnoses were able to be established in 80% of patients.[105] The causative factors in their study of 50 patients in order of frequency were cancer, chronic renal failure, viral pericarditis, systemic lupus erythematosus, rheumatoid arthritis, Dressler syndrome, tuberculosis, blunt chest trauma, and purulent pericarditis. No specific cause could be determined in 10 patients (20%).

Up to 9.8% of patients with a previous diagnosis of viral or **idiopathic pericarditis** are known to have recurrent pain without evidence of disease.[106] Previous use of corticosteroids and recurrent pericarditis were associated risk factors. After a 40-month follow-up, these patients were also noted to have an increased incidence of constrictive pericarditis. The probability of low-grade pericardial inflammation in these patients must be considered, and they require more frequent observation. The complete classification of pericarditis can be found in Table 11.1.

From a medical and forensic standpoint, the most important facet of pericarditis and pericardial effusion is, as for all aspects of disease, their recognition. It is important not to confuse acute pericarditis with acute myocardial infarction in evolution, or unstable angina, as the treatment of the

Table 11.1 Classification of Pericarditis

Clinical classification

- Acute pericarditis (<6 weeks)
  - Fibrinous
  - Effusive (serous or sanguineous)
- Subacute pericarditis (6 weeks to 6 months)
  - Effusive constrictive
  - Constrictive
- Chronic pericarditis (<6 months)
  - Constrictive
  - Effusive
  - Adhesive (nonconstrictive)

Etiologic classification

- Infectious pericarditis
  - Viral (coxsackievirus A and B, echovirus, mumps, adenovirus, hepatitis, HIV)
  - Pyogenic (pneumococcus, streptococcus, staphylococcus, *Neisseria, Legionella*)
  - Tuberculous
  - Fungal (histoplasmosis, coccidioidomycosis, *Candida*, blastomycosis)
  - Other infections (syphilitic, protozoal, parasitic)
- Noninfectious pericarditis
  - Acute myocardial infarction
  - Uremia
  - Neoplasia
    - Primary tumors (benign or malignant, mesothelioma)
    - Tumors metastatic to pericardium (lung and breast cancer, lymphoma, leukemia)
  - Myxedema
  - Cholesterol
  - Chylopericardium
  - Trauma
    - Penetrating chest wall
    - Nonpenetrating
  - Aortic dissection (with leakage into pericardial sac)
  - Postirradiation
  - Familial Mediterranean fever
  - Familial pericarditis
    - Mulibrey nanism*
  - Acute idiopathic
  - Whipple's disease
  - Sarcoidosis
- Pericarditis presumably related to hypersensitivity or autoimmunity
  - Rheumatic fever
  - Collagen vascular disease, (SLE, rheumatoid arthritis, ankylosing spondylitis, scleroderma, acute rheumatic fever, Wegener's granulomatosis

(*Continued*)

Table 11.1 (Continued)

Drug-induced (e.g., procainamide, hydralazine, phenytoin, isoniazide, minoxidil, anticoagulants, methysergide)
Postcardiac injury
Postmyocardial infarction (Dressler's syndrome)
Postpericardiotomy
Posttraumatic

Source: Braunwald, E., *Harrison's Principles of Internal Medicine*, 16th ed., McGraw-Hill, New York, 2005. With permission.

* An autosomal recessive syndrome, characterized by growth failure, muscle hypotonia, hepatomegaly, ocular changes, enlarged cerebral ventricles, mental retardation, and chronic constrictive pericarditis.

acute ischemic syndromes with anticoagulation and thrombolytic therapy is very dangerous in cases of pericarditis with or without effusion. Under these circumstances serious hemorrhagic pericardial effusion can occur, often with pericardial tamponade.

Equally as important, if not more so, is the prompt recognition and appropriate decision-making for the management of pericardial tamponade, regardless of etiology, as it can be the difference between life and death.

Pericardial effusion, either bland or hemorrhagic, can occur weeks or months after **blunt chest trauma**. It is usually nonhemorrhagic under these circumstances but can be serosanguineous. It is generally believed to be of similar etiology as the postcardiac injury syndrome or the **postpericardiotomy** syndrome, both of which are considered to be an antigenic immune response. More commonly occurring is the post-cardiac-surgery **pericardial effusion** because of the advent of continually increasing cardiac surgery and the use of anticoagulants. It was found to be present in 22% of 1,277 patients and was more frequent after coronary artery bypass surgery (CABG) than after valve replacement (25% vs. 17%). At approximately 30 days postsurgery, late tamponade occurred in 4% of patients, with a higher incidence after valve replacement surgery, undoubtedly associated with anticoagulation therapy.[107] The diagnosis of cardiac tamponade should be at the forefront of diagnostic possibilities in a postcardiotomy patient who shows signs of hemodynamic deterioration and low output failure. It can be preceded by very subtle signs or symptoms days or weeks following cardiac surgery. The incidence of pericardial tamponade following heart surgery has been variously stated as being from 0.3 to 2.1% in the earlier literature. Tamponade can occur in the absence of anticoagulation or during mild-intensity anticoagulation but usually occurs following intensive anticoagulation.

Pericardial tear (rupture) is almost always associated with other injuries to the heart or major blood vessels in cases of blunt cardiac trauma. Herniation of the heart through a large-sized tear can be urgently catastrophic, as the heart is, in effect, "choked to death." More often, a posttraumatic pericarditis with effusion is present and is usually of minor degree. If a laceration of the heart occurs, and the pericardium is intact, cardiac tamponade may ensue. This can be fatal in some cases with as little as 150 to 200 ml of blood in the pericardial sac. Immediate pericardiocentesis can be lifesaving if one can stop the bleeding into the sac—an uncommon circumstance in the author's experience. The same holds true for aortic dissection into the sac, a common cause of sudden death in these patients. The hemopericardium adversely affects the heart by restricting venous inflow into the right heart and by the mechanical interference to the ventricular contractility of both ventricles. If the pericardial sac is lacerated during the trauma, depending on the size of the laceration, either a more slowly developing hemopericardium will occur or none will occur at all, as the blood leaks into the mediastinum and pleural spaces, the latter producing hemorrhagic pleurisy, which may require thoracentesis. This situation is dependent upon the extent and location of the primary injury as well as the blood pool itself.

The diagnosis of pericarditis requires a clinical classification and an etiologic classification as noted in Table 11.1.

Valvular Heart Disease 12

Abnormalities of the heart valves are classified as congenital, infection-induced, inflammatory, degenerative, and traumatic. Toxic or drug-induced valvular disease may be included in the inflammatory category or is sometimes added as an additional category, noninfectious.

Traumatic tears and ruptures produce insufficiency of the valves involved and can affect any of the four valves singularly or in combination or their supportive structures (chordae or papillary muscle). Tears may occur in conjunction with myocardial contusion and other thoracic structural trauma, but can occur independently, dependent upon the type of physical trauma incurred. It has been stated that in patients who survive severe chest trauma, the aortic valve abnormality is the one most commonly encountered by the attending physician.[108] This is a debatable issue, as the occurrence of blunt chest trauma keeps increasing. The incidence of aortic valve trauma also increases in those who have sustained concomitant injuries to the aorta. Atrioventricular valve injuries are more common overall. They often coexist with fatal aortic or cardiac rupture.

When combined injuries of the aorta and aortic valve are excluded, the atrioventricular valve structures are most commonly traumatized and become insufficient, leading to mitral or tricuspid regurgitation, with neither being predominant.[109] Traumatic mitral or tricuspid insufficiency occurs usually as a result of rupture of the chordae tendineae or a papillary muscle. Traumatic rupture (laceration) of the atrioventricular valve leaflets (mitral or tricuspid) is a less frequent cause of valvular insufficiency than rupture of a chordae or papillary muscle. In either situation, prompt medical therapy is usually necessary, and in most cases, surgical intervention is required. Traumatic valve lacerations may occur in the absence of myocardial contusion and blunt cardiac trauma and is the result of the increased hydrostatic pressure in a blood-filled cardiac chamber produced by abdominal or thoracic crushing injuries. Combined mitral and tricuspid valve rupture has been reported following a fall of only 5 feet.[109] Veeragandham[110] reported an unusually rare combination of posttraumatic tricuspid insufficiency and left ventricular aneurysm in a 9-year-old boy, which were successfully corrected by surgery.

It should be noted that atrial fibrillation caused by traumatic tricuspid insufficiency can occur shortly following the traumatic insult or can develop many years later (several months to 20 years).[111] The latter phenomenon is extremely uncommon.

Although surgical correction of posttraumatic tricuspid insufficiency has been reported from 10 to as long as 46 years later, it has been suggested that with the operative techniques currently available, earlier intervention is preferable. This not only alleviates symptoms, but more importantly, prevents progressive right ventricular dysfunction.[112]

Rheumatic heart disease has become less frequent in the highly developed industrial world and is being replaced by congenital and genetically induced valvular disease. Primary endocarditis-induced valvular disease has become more common in the current era of illicit drug use. These may be caused by a variety of bacterial and fungal agents, however *Staphylococcus aureus* is the usual culprit under these circumstances.

The commonest example of genetically-induced valvular disease is **mitral prolapse**, a myxomatous degeneration of the valve substance, which produces varying degrees of mitral insufficiency. The tricuspid valve may also be affected singularly or in combination, producing tricuspid insufficiency and right heart strain. The mitral or tricuspid insufficiency caused by a **prolapsed valve** can vary from being totally insignificant to hemodynamically insignificant to moderate or severe. The degree of insufficiency (regurgitation) is dependent upon the degree of pathology and the duration of the disease. Rupture of a chordae tendinae can occur in more advanced cases. This can be a catastrophic event requiring immediate medical and surgical intervention. If clinically detectable valvular insufficiency is present, bacterial endocarditis prophylaxis is generally recommended.

Cardiac arrhythmias are a less frequent accompaniment of mitral prolapse, and when they occur are usually supraventricular in origin. Pseudoanginal chest discomfort and vague, nondescript chest pains have also been frequently described. Sudden cardiac death, although reported, is extremely rare. The latter is more common in cases of advanced **aortic stenosis**. It is probable that in the developed industrialized nations a congenitally bicuspid aortic valve is now a more common cause of aortic stenosis than is rheumatic aortic stenosis. The stenosis in these cases is due to progressive calcific degeneration of the aortic valve cusps and annulus. Signs or symptoms may not occur until the sixth decade of life and progress accordingly. A commonly overlooked etiology of aortic stenosis in the elderly is that of calcific degenerative valvular disease, which affects the aortic annulus as well as the valve leaflets. As in any valvular pathology, the timing of surgery is of utmost importance.

Aortic valve areas of 1 cm^2 or less and gradients of greater than 55 mm Hg are generally felt to be the points of strong consideration for surgical intervention of one type or another, usually valve replacement when feasible. Symptoms may occur in patients with a smaller or larger degree of stenosis. The most common are cardiac arrhythmia, dizziness, syncope, dyspnea, angina pectoris, and congestive heart failure. In cases of aortic stenosis in adults, cardiac catheterization is done prior to surgical decision-making to assess the status of the coronary circulation. Any of these signs or symptoms are warnings of impending disaster if not promptly and appropriately managed. Clinical studies have shown quite clearly that it is prudent to begin therapeutic intervention prior to the occurrence of symptoms. This holds true for any valvular dysfunction. The mechanism of sudden death in aortic stenosis is stated as being due to coronary insufficiency caused by outflow obstruction in combination with myocardial insufficiency produced by the long-standing stress and strain placed upon the coronary flow-restricted myocardium. Sometimes calcific occlusion around the coronary ostia may also be present, producing signs and symptoms associated with coronary insufficiency.

A rare cause of recurrent stroke syndrome has been associated with a valvular degenerative condition known as **Lambl's excrescences**. These are frond-like lesions of 1 to several millimeters in size (rarely coalescing to larger lesions) that occur on the valve margins and are known to deteriorate and cause thromboembolic episodes to various organs in addition to those related to the production of cerebral ischemic episodes. These have been treated by combination anticoagulation or, in recurrent cases, surgical excision. It is believed that they are produced by normal trauma of valve closure. Transesophageal echocardiography is generally necessary for evaluating these cases.

Non-infective endocarditis (marantic endocarditis) may occur on the valve surfaces in association with various chronic disease states, such as cancer, tuberculosis, and uremia. These lesions differ from those of Lambl's excrescences in that they contain platelets and fibrin, which may embolize. These lesions may become secondarily infected and lead to the development of acute or subacute infective endocarditis.

Another form of noninfective endocarditis known as **Libman–Sacks endocarditis** is known to occur in patients with systemic lupus erythematosus and antiphospholipid syndrome, which typically are found on the underside of the mitral valve leaflets.

Cardiac Tumors 13

Primary neoplasms of the heart are extremely rare, and, when present, the majority are benign. **Sarcomas** are the most frequent primary malignancy to affect the heart, whereas **myxomas** are the most frequent primary cardiac tumors to affect the heart at all ages. Some may be familial, but most are not. Females predominate the incidence at all ages. When present, most myxomas will involve the left atrium and, next in frequency, the right atrium. Signs and symptoms may be absent but when clinically diagnosed may erroneously present as a case of primary mitral stenosis and/or mitral regurgitation. The more uncommon ventricular myxomas may cause either left- or right-sided subvalvular obstruction. Myxomas may be misdiagnosed as bacterial endocarditis because of their propensity to cause fever, rash, arthralgias, anemia, elevated erythrocyte sedimentation rate, and increased or decreased platelet counts. Diagnostic procedures involve echocardiography, CT, or MRI scans and at times, cardiac catheterization, now done less frequently except when complicating factors are suspected or to exclude coronary artery disease in appropriate patients. Treatment is surgical excision, but myxomas are known to recur in up to 2% of sporadic cases and up to 20% in familial cases. **Cardiac lipomas** are relatively common, often very large, and usually detected at autopsy. **Myxomatous degeneration** of the atrioventricular valves should not be confused with atrial or ventricular myxomas and are two distinct pathologic processes. **Papillary fibroelastomas** are next in frequency in the adult population. In children, rhabdomyomas and fibromas are more common.

Side effects that have been attributed to cardiac papillary fibroelastomas have been related to stroke, pulmonary embolism, transient cerebral ischemic attacks, angina, myocardial infarction, heart failure, syncope, and sudden death.[113] Successful surgical excision of a double papillary fibroelastoma of the aortic valve in an asymptomatic elderly man without the need of valve replacement has been reported.[114] Schoondyke et al. reported excision of a papillary fibroelastoma of the left ventricular wall in an elderly woman.[115] The tumor was discovered by transthoracic echocardiography performed because the patient presented with a cardiac murmur that was previously not present. Shing and Rubenson reported surgical excision of a papillary fibroelastoma of the mitral valve in a 34-year-old male hospitalized for a major embolic stroke.[116] The tumor was discovered by transesophageal echocardiography performed to investigate the possible embolic sources that can cause stroke and illustrate the importance of the diagnostic studies utilized for this purpose.

Papillary fibroelastomas are the commonest cardiac valve tumors.[117] The onset of new murmurs, unexplained embolic events, and otherwise unexplained cardiac complications may be clues as to the presence of papillary fibroelastomas or other cardiac tumors. If suspicion is high, one must go beyond routine transthoracic echocardiography and proceed to transesophageal echocardiography because of its greater sensitivity for detecting certain valvular abnormalities. Intramyocardial tumors (usually **hemangiomas and mesotheliomas**) are small, and may cause serious conduction defects and, rarely, sudden death.

Carcinoid tumors usually originate in the distal ileum and vary in their degree of malignancy. Other primary sites are the bronchial tubes, ovaries, stomach, thyroid, large intestine, pancreas, and appendix. Those arising within the appendix rarely produce metastases. When present, metastases occur mainly to the liver, lung, pancreas, ovaries, adrenal glands, and less commonly to the brain and heart. They are mentioned here because of their great propensity for developing cardiac valvular abnormalities, mainly on the right side of the heart, but left-sided lesions are known to occur. Right-sided lesions include tricuspid insufficiency and pulmonic stenosis and insufficiency. Left-sided lesions are those of mitral insufficiency and aortic insufficiency and aortic stenosis. Damage to the valves occurs because of their exposure to noxious substances secreted by the tumor and can lead to heart failure, tachycardia, and angina pectoris. Vasospastic angina in the absence of cardiac valvular abnormalities may also occur. Carcinoid symptoms in general are flushing, severe spasmodic abdominal pain, and relentless diarrhea, up to 30 times daily. Marked hypotension and shock can also occur. The diagnosis is made on the basis of finding an elevated level of the serotonin metabolite 5-hydroxyindolacetic acid (5-HIAA) in the urine, increased serum serotonin levels, and a positive radioactive octreotide imaging scan.[118]

Schoen et al. reported a patient with typical exertional angina pectoris secondary to metastatic infiltration of the myocardium by a large cell **non-Hodgkin's lymphoma**.[119] The ECG demonstrated ischemic type ST-T changes. Echocardiography revealed a pericardial effusion and apical hypokinesia. Coronary angiography was unremarkable. The chest pain, myocardial mass, and ST-segment depression all resolved following chemotherapy.

14 Cardiomyopathic Disorders

Cardiomyopathy (heart muscle disease) may be broadly classified as being specific (factor or organism related) or idiopathic (unknown etiology). Currently, the latter is the commonest cause of difficult to diagnose cardiomyopathy and is believed to be related to a previous and unrecognized viral inflammation of the heart (myocarditis) with or without a subsequent autoimmune effect. Viral illness is also the commonest cause of myocarditis as well as pericarditis not involved in the progression to viral cardiomyopathy. Cardiomyopathy may be classified according to known, specific causative factors, or idiopathic and genetically induced abnormalities. Pathophysiologically, they can also be further subclassified into dilated, congestive, restrictive, hypertrophic, and ischemic varieties.

Ischemic cardiomyopathy is now being frequently diagnosed as a concomitant aftermath of severe, multivessel coronary arterial insufficiency, myocardial infarction, myocardial fibrosis, and chronic heart failure. Used in these terms, it naturally becomes the commonest and most frequently diagnosed cause under the heading of cardiomyopathy. It seems preferable to define the end result of myocardial ischemia secondary to diffuse coronary disease and its consequences as advanced coronary arterial insufficiency, preterminal or terminal, with the addition of the end result—chronic angina, cardiac decompensation, or chronic heart failure. This relegates the original use of the term *cardiomyopathy* to the more specific, as well as the ill-defined, causes of heart muscle disease, whether they affect primarily the heart muscle (myocytes), the supporting structures, or genetically-induced electro-physiologic anomalies. If a specific cause is determined, it is added to the general classification. If the specific cause is unknown, idiopathic is added to the pathophysiologic type or diagnosis. *Ischemic cardiomyopathy* is becoming a commonplace diagnostic term due to the increasing longevity of survival of coronary atherosclerotic patients. This in turn is due to the vast improvements in pharmacotherapy and invasive mechanical procedures.

There appears to be a strong genetic predisposing pattern to the various "inherited" types of cardiomyopathy as well as in those individuals predisposed to the severe forms of viral cardiomyopathy. This includes the various forms of arrhythmogenic dysplasias affecting the right ventricle, the ventricular apices, prolonged QT syndromes, and Brugada syndrome.

In addition, the terms **diabetic cardiomyopathy** and **syndrome X** are slowly achieving diagnostic consideration and acceptability. In some diabetic patients, there appears to be an inherent cardiac muscle dysfunction as well as small blood vessel disease not associated with macrovascular atherosclerotic disease of significance. Similarly, in syndrome X, a malfunction of the arteriolar–capillary system appears to be present, in which true angina pectoris occurs. It may or may not be associated with ECG abnormalities at rest or during exercise and can be relieved by nitrates and other anti-anginal therapies, principally the calcium channel blockers.

Brugada syndrome refers to patients who present with a right bundle branch block pattern on the ECG, persistent ST elevation in leads V1 to V3 with a "saddle-back" configuration, and are predisposed to polymorphic ventricular tachycardia and sudden death. Ventricular tachycardia deteriorating to ventricular fibrillation is the most probable cause of sudden death.[120,121,122] Cases reported as the Brugada syndrome with right ventricular conduction defects (incomplete right bundle branch block) have been described in the medical literature and are exemplified by the persistent ST-segment elevation in leads V1 to V3. These patients apparently have the same predisposition toward the development of ventricular tachycardia, ventricular fibrillation, presyncope, syncope, and sudden death. An etiologic **classification of myocarditis** is noted in Table 14.1. These extensive etiologic factors may or may not lead to the development of cardiomyopathy. In addition, the associated cardiomyopathy, when present, can be self-limited or halted in its progression. Under appropriate circumstances and therapy, it may be curable.

Myocarditis and cardiomyopathy may be progressive or may go into remission with minor pathologic effects, depending on the cause and measures taken to alleviate the basic pathology.

Restrictive cardiomyopathy implies a restriction of right and left ventricular filling with normal or reduced volumes and normal or near normal systolic function. It may be infiltrative or noninfiltrative, as seen in cases of coronary insufficiency or hypertension, and commonly produces diastolic dysfunction and heart failure. Restrictive cardiomyopathy is generally seen in the following disease states:

1. Chronic ischemic heart disease
2. Chronic hypertensive cardiovascular disease
3. Amyloidosis
4. Hemochromatosis
5. Sarcoidosis
6. Glycogen storage disease and its metabolic counterparts
7. Eosinophilic syndrome
8. Carcinoid syndrome
9. Scleroderma (progressive systemic)

Table 14.1 Etiologic Factors in the Causation of Myocarditis and Cardiomyopathy

Infections
Viral
Bacterial
Rickettsial
Protozoal
Fungal
Spirochetal
Parasitic
Inflammatory
Rheumatoid–collagen disease
Kawasaki syndrome
Allergic reactions
Chemical toxins
Infiltrative and metabolic disorders
Hypothyroidism
Amyloidosis
Sarcoidosis
Neoplasms (primary and secondary)
Congenital and genetically induced metabolic disorders
Miscellaneous
Contraceptive drugs
Cocaine
Radiation therapy
Pharmacologic agents
Pregnancy
Tachycardia (incessant, refractory)

The most commonly accepted etiology of the most frequently encountered **congestive-dilated cardiomyopathy** is a viral illness producing varying stages of acute, subacute, and chronic myocarditis, the latter leading to presumed auto-immune inflammatory changes before becoming quiescent, leaving the heart with severe postinflammatory destruction and fibrosis. The more common viruses involved are adenovirus, enterovirus (Coxsackie B), cytomegalovirus, parovirus, echovirus, and arborvirus. In fact, almost any type of virus may be implicated. The HIV virus is known to cause diffuse myocarditis. Other common viruses such as the hepatitis, influenza, and Epstein-Barr (infectious mononucleosis) may occasionally be implicated. The viruses involved in causing measles, mumps, chickenpox, smallpox and rabies are more uncommonly involved. The role of respiratory syncytial virus is not, as yet, well-defined.

The foci of the damage may be repetitively localized or extremely diffuse. The end result causes the various clinical findings, including heart failure, cardiac arrhythmias of all types, conduction defects, depolarization and repolarization abnormalities on the ECG (infarct-like Q waves, bundle branch and AV blocks, nonspecific intraventricular conduction defects and ischemic-type ST-T abnormalities).

This disease may produce massive cardiomegaly and severe, unremitting congestive heart failure with a marked predisposition toward cardiac arrhythmias and sudden death. Valvular dysfunction and mural thrombus formation with a subsequent high incidence of embolic events is a frequent accompaniment.

The myocarditis produced by various viral agents may be acute and self-limited or can revert to a less-well-understood subacute stage that can progress to a chronic and unreparative stage of stable myopathy or may progress to an unstable state of advanced cardiomyopathy terminating in congestive heart failure, dysrhythmia, and death. At this stage cardiac transplantation remains the only effective form of therapy. **Viral myocarditis and cardiomyopathy** can be clinically quite obscure and pathologically indistinct. In rare instances, sudden death may occur before the disease is diagnosable by routine clinical tests. In fact, even with careful routine anatomic and microscopic study following a thorough autopsy examination, the diagnosis may be difficult to confirm.

It is generally accepted at present that idiopathic dilated cardiomyopathy has a 50% familial incidence. Small to large transmural scars may be present in the cases of advanced idiopathic dilated cardiomyopathy in the presence of normal epicardial arteries. Intracardiac thrombi are said to occur in approximately 50% of patients, necessitating therapy with anticoagulants. A chromosomal genetic abnormality producing immune regulatory dysfunction is being investigated. It is felt that the inciting factor inducing this abnormality, which leads to an autoimmune phenomenon, is initiated by a virus. Therapy with corticosteroids has generally shown no benefit, even when added to or combined with various other immune-suppressive therapy, the latter also of doubtful benefit. The last therapeutic option at present is cardiac transplantation. Table 14.2 presents a list of genetically induced cardiomyopathies. It remains to be seen as to which of these diagnoses are purely hereditable or are triggered by an extraneous source (i.e., viral).

Peripartum cardiomyopathy can present as a slowly progressive or sudden state of cardiac decompensation, usually during the last trimester of pregnancy or the first few months postpartum. As many as 50% of cases are found to be self-limiting and can go on to nearly complete resolution or complete resolution and permanent remission. Coronary emboli have been rarely reported.[123]

Toxic cardiomyopathy can occur as a result of exposure to many chemical agents, various pharmacotherapeutic drugs, and environmental toxins. Some

Table 14.2 Genetically Associated Idiopathic Cardiopathies

Idiopathic hypertrophic subaortic stenosis
Nonobstructive septal hypertrophy
Apical cardiomyopathy
Arrhythmogenic right ventricular dysplasia
Idiopathic dilated cardiomyopathy
Familial cardiomyopathy
Mitochondrial cardiomyopathy
Endocardial fibroelastosis
Cardiopathies associated with numerous heredo-familial neuromuscular dystrophies and metabolic disorders
Long QT syndrome (an electrophysiologic conduction disorder)
Short QT syndrome (an electrophysiologic channel disorder)

substances produce predominantly a form of myocarditis, producing cardiac dysrrhythmia and ECG abnormalities, whereas others cause myocardial depression, heart failure, and sudden death. Some of the more common agents involved are cocaine, cobalt, lithium, chloroquine, phenothiazines, interferon, lead, methysergide, interleukin, various industrial hydrocarbons, and, occasionally, antibiotics. These are briefly reviewed in the following chapter.

Chronic alcohol abuse can cause a progressive, stable, or remitting cardiomyopathy, the latter dependent upon the extent of the overall damage incurred and the state and logistics of alcohol ingestion in terms of quality, quantity, and discontinuation or continuation. Its features are similar to those of idiopathic (viral) cardiomyopathy but generally not as severe as progressive idiopathic dilated cardiomyopathy. Paroxysms of atrial fibrillation are often the first clue to its presence, although any cardiac arrhythmia may occur, as well as unexpected congestive heart failure. Grand mal epileptic seizures are not uncommon in these cases and can occur independently or can exacerbate an underlying epileptic or preepileptic state. A list of the most common genetically–associated cardiomyopathies is reviewed in Table 14.2.

Long QT syndrome is caused by a disturbance in the electrophysiologic function of the specific electrolyte channels within the myocardial cells, and to date has been associated with at least 10 types of genetic disorders, often familial. These types vary in severity and response to medical therapy and can be associated with presyncope or syncope caused by ventricular arrhythmias. Sudden death is known to occur. Aggravation of these disorders has been shown to be associated with the use of certain medications (antibiotics, psychotherapeutic drugs, cardiac drugs, antihistamines, immunomodulating agents, antifungal drugs, and some chemical toxins).

Cardiomyopathy due to severe, prolonged **iron deficiency** has been more recently appreciated. The basic underlying pathophysiologic mechanism of its production is yet to be defined.[124] It is said to respond to or reverse itself with iron replacement.

The **parasitic tapeworm** *Echinococcus granulosus* can affect the liver, lungs, and heart (hydatid cyst disease). It infests the gut of dogs and is transmitted to humans via infected vegetables and water. Surgical removal of the cysts is generally recommended.[125]

The antineoplastic drug **doxorubicin (an anthracycline)** is well known for its cardiac toxicity and its proclivity for the development of **drug-induced cardiomyopathy**. It has been reported that the prophylactic use of carvedilol may protect against the development of cardiac decompensation secondary to systolic and diastolic dysfunction in these patients.[126,127] The use of **angiotensin-converting enzyme inhibitors** in patients undergoing high-dose chemotherapy has been stated as being protective against the development and progression of left ventricular dysfunction.[127]

Toxic and Physical Influences

V

Cardiotoxicity 15

General Pharmacologic and Physical Overview

Cardiovascular toxicology is a subspecialty in itself. The substances that can affect the heart are legion and include commonly used pharmacologic drugs, numerous industrial solvents and propellants, organic and inorganic compounds, plants and plant products, industrial pollution, outdoor air pollution, alcohol, and cigarette smoke. Some of the commonest offenders and their predominant effects will be briefly outlined in this chapter. Table 15.1 lists common offending agents producing a true toxic cardiomyopathy. Table 15.2 lists drugs that are more frequently known to produce an inflammatory reaction (hypersensitivity- induced myocarditis). Both tables are only partial listings of the more common substances that produce cardiac toxicity.

The commonest medically induced cardiomyopathies are those due to cancer chemotherapy. It is common knowledge that left ventricular function due to the anthracycline class drugs decreases as the dosage of these drugs increases. Furthermore, it may not be possible to prevent congestive heart failure far enough in advance of a therapeutic drug schedule so that adjustment and avoidance of cardiac decompensation can be accomplished. Whenever possible, patients with known cardiac decompensation (heart dysfunction without clinical signs of heart failure) should receive drugs known to be less toxic to the myocardium. Routine electrocardiography, echocardiography, and radionuclide assessment of left ventricular function (MUGA scan) can be helpful in selecting and following these patients. Sequential studies are the rule and must be carefully interpreted and followed accordingly. Patients with ejection fractions of 50% or less must be more closely followed with repeat studies than those with ejection fractions of 55% or greater. It is generally unwise to administer a cardiotoxic agent to patients with ejection fractions of 30% or lower. A decrease in the left ventricular ejection fraction of 10% or more should signal the end of utilizing the particular offending agent indefinitely.

Digitalis preparations are plant-derived cardiac glycosides. The commonest preparation in use is digoxin. Serum digoxin levels above 2 ng/ml are considered abnormal, but may or may not be toxic, depending on clinical circumstances. In certain situations, that is, atrial fibrillation, levels needed to produce slowing of the heart rate by producing adequate atrioventricular block may sometimes require levels of 2.5 ng/ml or higher, without evidence of clinical or

Table 15.1 Representative Examples of Substances Known to Produce Toxic Cardiac Effects

Alcohol[a]
Amphetamines[a]
Anticancer agents (daunorubicin, doxorubicin, cyclophosphamide, 5-fluorouracil)
Antiretroviral drugs (zidovudine, dideoxyinosine, etc.)
Antimony
Arsenic[a]
Barbiturates
Cobalt[a]
Cocaine[a]
Carbon monoxide[a]
Catecholamines (in excess)
Chloroquine
Emetine
Hydrocarbons[a]
Interferon alpha
Interleukin
Lead
Lithium
Mercury
Methysergide
Paraquat
Phosphorous
Thallium
Thioridazine-type drugs

[a] Reversible or partially reversible.

electrophysiologic toxicity. Digoxin and its counterparts (digitalis leaf, digitoxin, ouabain) may produce any type of cardiac arrhythmia. It should be noted that **postmortem digoxin levels** are inaccurately high because it is released from body tissues into the blood following death. Analysis for digoxin must be performed on the vitreous humor of the eye if one finds the assessment necessary.

Arsenic is a tasteless, odorless, and highly poisonous substance, which has been used in herbicides, pesticides, and wood preservatives and in the electronics industry. It can be found in all living organisms. The average daily human intake varies from 0.5 to 1.0mg/day, usually from ingesting food and water. Death from arsenic is rarely sudden, can be rapid (several hours), and can be prolonged and agonizing, the latter a hallmark of **thallium poisoning**. Many investigative historians believe that the infamous Napoleon Bonaparte was murdered by being given repetitive doses of arsenic.

ECG changes may be seen as prolongation of the QT interval and ST-T changes. A sensory–motor neuropathy is almost always present. The heart, liver,

Table 15.2 Drugs Reported to Cause Hypersensitivity Cardiomyopathy (Toxic Myocarditis)

Drug class	Drugs
Antibiotics	Ampicillin, penicillin, streptomycin, sulfadiazine, sulfisoxazole, tetracycline, chloramphenicol, amphotericin, erythromycin
Antihypertensives	Chlorthalidone,[a] hydrochlorothiazide,[a] methyl dopa
Antiepileptics	Carbamazepine, phenindione, phenytoin
Anti-infectives	Isoniazid, paraminosalicylic acid
Antipsychotics	Amitriptyline
Miscellaneous	Sulfonylureas, acetazolamide

[a] Diuretic class.

Table 15.3 Side-effects of Tricyclic Antidepressants

Clinical
Sinus tachycardia
Hypotension (especially orthostatic)
Left ventricular dysfunction
ECG changes
ST-T abnormality
Prolonged QT interval
Prolonged PR interval
Prolonged QRS interval
Intraventricular conduction defects
Cardiac arrhythmia

and kidneys may be affected. Survivors of an acute ingestion of arsenic develop white, horizontal bands in the fingernails several months later (Mee's lines).

Psychotropic drugs of all types are known to have varying effects on the heart, most often prolongation of the QT interval. The **tricyclic antidepressants** have been one of the commonest class of drugs known to have the potential for producing significant untoward effects on the cardiovascular system. Caution is warranted in prescribing these drugs in patients with known cardiovascular disease. Careful patient selection and appropriate monitoring is warranted, and includes monitoring blood pressure, pulse, electrocardiographic changes, and at times,sometimes ventricular function. Table 15.3 lists known side effects. The "tricyclics" are also known to have antiarrhythmic as well as arrhythmic potential because of their quinidine-like effect. It is preferable to avoid using these drugs with class I antiarrhytmic agents (quinidine, procainamide, disopyramide).

The newer classes of antidepressants reportedly have fewer cardiovascular side effects. Cumulative evidence suggests that **maprotaline** has the potential for side effects similar to the tricyclics. **Amoxapine, trazodone** and **fluoxetine** have side effects of lesser degrees of severity and incidence than other antidepressants.

The **antipsychotic drugs** of the **phenothiazine** group are known to cause tachycardia, orthostatic hypotension, prolonged QT interval, T wave changes, and intraventricular conduction defects.

The anti-cancer drugs **doxorubicin** and **daurotobicin** can produce well-recognized changes in the ST-T and QRS segments. A decrease in the voltage of the QRS complex portends the development of cardiomyopathy, but is not always apparent. When it does occur, it is usually too late to be of significant value in reversing the cardiomyopathy on discontinuance of the drug. Heart failure has been reported in nearly 10% of patients receiving these drugs, and more than 20% of patients are found to have a decrease in the left ventricular ejection fraction (LVEF) at some point during or following completion of therapy. It is generally believed that some degree of chronic cardiomyopathy will develop in all patients given **anthracyclines** and that either right or left ventricular dysfunction may predominate. It is now accepted practice to obtain several measurements of left ventricular function at appropriate time intervals when using these drugs. Serious left ventricular dysfunction can occur within days after using **doxorubicin** or weeks, months, or more than one year later. One must therefore watch these patients closely during their clinical follow-up—not only during therapy but for some time thereafter. Asymptomatic children who were previously treated with an anthracycline were found to have decreased myocardial systolic reserve after exercise.

Most other chemotherapeutic agents such as **5-fluorouracil, vincristine, vindesine, cyclophosphamide, mitoxantrone, and amsacrine** vary in their individual propensity for cardiotoxic effects (Table 15.4). The risk of cardiovascular disease caused by various modalities involved in the treatment of breast cancer is finally being recognized and appreciated. In addition to abnormalities that may be produced by radiation therapy, the short- and long-term cardiovascular risks of adjuvant chemotherapy of the numerous agents involved are listed in the Appendix B.

Table 15.4 Cardiac Side Effects of Some Chemotherapeutic Drugs

Drug	Side effect
5 Fluorouracil	Ischemia, infarction, heart failure, arrhythmia, sudden death; some adverse events believed to be due to coronary spasm and coagulopathic dysfunction
Vinca alkaloids	Angina, infarction, hypotension
Cyclophosphamide	Myocardial necrosis
Mitoxantrone	Heart failure, myocardial fibrosis
Amsacrine	Arrhythmias, prolonged QT interval, heart failure, sudden death

Patients receiving **oral contraceptives** are known to have an increased incidence of thromboembolic events, stroke, myocardial infarction, and hypertension. The more recent formulations of these drugs have decreased the incidence of adverse effects, but caution is advised when other risk factors are known or suspected. These include the presence of cardiovascular disease, history of previous thromboembolic events, smoking, hypertension, and diabetes. Suspicion of a genetically induced coagulopathic disorder (factor V Leiden defect, protein C, protein S, and antithrombiin III deficiencies) should be fully investigated when appropriate.

Successful treatment of **doxorubicin-induced cardiomyopathy** following the administration of carvedilol has been reported.[126,127,128] Transient **effusive-constrictive pericarditis** due to chemotherapy with cytarabine and daunorubicin in patients with acute myelogenous leukemia is known to rarely occur.[129] **Chemotherapy-induced pericarditis** is uncommon but has been reported with several chemotherapeutic agents. **Anaphylactic-induced myocardial injury** caused by a systemic reaction to **ampicillin** and **sulbactam** has also been reported.[130] These patients may sustain acute myocardial injury in spite of having normal coronary arteries on angiography.

Toxic myocarditis without myocardial necrosis can result from numerous insults and exposures: drugs, chemicals, insect bites and stings, various environmental exposures, and ingestion of members of the plant kingdom.

Drug-induced heart failure can be precipitated by chemotherapeutic agents, anti-arrhythmic drugs, beta-adrenoceptor antagonists, nonsteroidal anti-inflammatory drugs, calcium channel blocking drugs, anesthetic agents, antidepressants, and immunomodulating drugs (interferons, interleukins).

Cocaine

Cocaine use (abuse) has, unfortunately, become quite prevalent in our society. It has a half-life of 50 to 90 minutes and produces a sensation of euphoria for 30 minutes when smoked or up to 1½ hours when snorted. It is metabolized by the liver and excreted in the urine. Metabolites can be found in the urine for 2 or more days after its use. ECG effects can include conduction defects and increases in the PR, QRS, and QT intervals similar to those caused by anti-arrhythmic drugs. Cocaine blocks the reuptake of catecholamines at the presynaptic levels and the peripheral nervous system, and enhances the release of catecholamines from central and peripheral stores, causing tachycardia, hypertension, hyperthermia, and mydriasis. It causes contraction of diseased and normal coronary arteries and has a direct toxic effect on the myocardium, as well as adverse effects on endothelial function and the coagulation mechanism. It causes damage to the coronary arteries and enhances

Table 15.5 Common Complications of Cocaine Use

Sudden death
Myocardial infarction
Cardiac arrhythmias
Cardiomyopathy (acute and chronic)
Hypertension
Electrocardiographic abnormalities
Stroke
Pulmonary hemorrhage
Acute aortic dissection
Acute peripheral muscle damage

the development of atherosclerosis, thereby adding to its propensity for producing myocardial infarction, sudden death, and stroke (Table 15.5).

Chest pain associated with cocaine use may be due to vasospastic angina, coronary occlusion, plaque rupture of any size coronary artery or arteriole, or dissection of the aorta. Micro-infarcts of variable degree may occur and may not be readily detectable by the usual cardiac enzyme analyses.

Cocaine toxicity can cause significant rhabdomyolysis, so one should investigate any CPK and CK-MB enzyme elevations by using a troponin I assay, or use the troponin I assay as a primary test for myocardial damage. Severe rhabdomyolysis can cause acute renal failure, necessitating observation of serum creatinine levels. The treatment of cardiovascular complications secondary to cocaine abuse is similar to other cardiac pathologic states (unstable angina, myocardial infarction, cardiac arrhythmia, and heart failure). Emphasis is placed on the use of nitrates, calcium channel blockers, aspirin, and other anticoagulants, keeping in mind the high propensity toward the development of hemorrhagic stroke in these individuals. The use of beta-blocking drugs should be avoided because of the possibility of enhanced vasoconstriction produced by beta-blockade. Use of class I anti-arrhythmic drugs for the treatment of sustained and nonsustained arrhythmias should be avoided.

It is accepted fact that illicit drug use is a significant predictor of cardiovascular complications in the first 6 months after coronary artery bypass grafting.[131] It has been stated that **methamphetamine abuse** is the most widespread illicit drug used in the United States. Khung-Keong and colleagues concluded that after adjustment of various risk factors (coronary artery disease, hypertension, diabetes, cigarette smoking, alcohol abuse, marijuana use, and cocaine use), young individuals using amphetamines had a diagnostic prevalence for cardiomyopathy of 3.7 times compared to controls. They noted that previous studies concluded that methamphetamine use can be associated with structural and functional damage to cardiac myocytes, causing chemical manifestations of cardiomyopathy, including congestive heart failure.[132]

Alcohol

Alcohol in significant daily amounts or heavy binge drinking can cause or aggravate hypertension, heart failure, and cardiac arrhythmias and can cause sudden death. It is one of the foremost causative factors in the production of secondary cardiomyopathy. If a cardiomyopathy due to alcohol is suspected early in the course of treatment, cessation of alcohol consumption can halt the progression of the disease and may reverse the abnormality to near normal, just as in the evolution of alcohol-induced hepatitis and early cirrhosis. Alcohol has a direct toxic effect on the myocardium and conduction tissue as well as an inherent effect due to nutritional deficiencies produced by alcoholism. **Cobalt-induced cardiomyopathy** has been eliminated since breweries stopped using cobalt for the purpose of maintaining a "good head of foam." Cardiovascular complications caused by alcohol include ventricular dilatation, left- and right-sided heart failure, atrial fibrillation, elevated diastolic blood pressure secondary to peripheral vasoconstriction, heart block, arrhythmic sudden death, and varying types and degrees of embolic phenomena.

Physical Agents

Cardiac toxicity secondary to **insect bites and stings** has been reported involving scorpions, black widow spiders, wasps, and ticks. Abnormalities produced have been associated with basic ECG changes and arrhythmias and the more seriously morbid and fatal events of circulatory collapse, myocardial infarction, heart failure, and sudden death. Sustained atrial flutter and atrial fibrillation following bee stings is known to occur.

Plant-induced cardiotoxicity is a relatively well-known but often forgotten manifestation of nature, similar to that produced by cardiac glycosides. The plants in question include oleander, lily of the valley, milkweed, and various berry plants.

Larkspur is known to cause myocardial depression, hypotension, and cardiac dysrhythmias because of its aconitine composition. Jimsonweed and night blossom plants have anticholinergic effects. Castor beans can cause hypotension and circulatory collapse. Mistletoe is also known to cause marked hypertension because of its amine constituents. The use of **Chinese herbs** containing aconite alkaloids has been reported as causing ventricular tachycardia leading to ventricular fibrillation and death.

Coronary artery spasm complicating anaphylaxis caused by application of the **skin disinfectant chlorhexidine** was reported in a patient who had angiographically normal coronary arteries.[133]

Numerous **industrial solvents** and **propellants**, especially those of the halogenated class, are known to produce cardiac effects and central nervous system irritability. Cardiac arrhythmias, ST-T changes, myocardial depression, sudden death, and various pulmonary effects have been described.

Androgenic Steroids

The increased prevalence of **anabolic-androgenic steroid** use by athletes and those who desire a "quick-fix" to improving their physique is cause for considerable concern. Anabolic (androgenic) steroids are available in many natural and synthetic forms and are usually easily obtainable. Adverse effects of these substances include cardiotoxicity, liver toxicity, liver tumors (benign and malignant), lipid abnormalities, infertility, psychologic dysfunction, decreased immune function, and masculinization in women.[134] The **cardiovascular effects of androgenic drugs** based on pathophysiologic dysfunction and their subsequent clinical effects are noted in Table 15.6.

Table 15.6 Cardiovascular Effects of Androgenic/Anabolic Steroids

Lipid metabolic dysfunction
Decreased HDL
Increased LDL
Increased hepatic triglyceride lipase activity
Atherogenesis and plaque formation
Enhanced activity of the coagulation system
Endothelial dysfunction
Platelet aggregation
Increased levels of intrinsic and extrinsic coagulation factors
Increased coronary vessel reactivity (vasospasm)
Coronary thrombosis
Hypertension
Left ventricular hypertrophy
Diastolic dysfunction
Direct myocardial injury
Cardiomegaly
Myocardial infarction
Myocardial fibrosis
Cardiomyopathy
Cardiac dysrhythmia
Sudden cardiac death

Carbon Monoxide

The primary physiologic effect of carbon monoxide (CO) on the body is its high affinity for hemoglobin, which produces tissue hypoxia. The end result is determined by the concentration and time of exposure, an individual's hemoglobin content, and the presence of coronary heart disease or previous heart muscle damage. Acute poisoning can cause ST-T abnormalities on the ECG and supraventricular or ventricular dysrrhythmia. Patients who have coronary artery disease are more likely to sustain angina pectoris, and near-fatal exposure has been reported as causing myocardial necrosis and cardiomyopathy in persons without coronary occlusion. Cardiac effects may appear acutely or may be delayed for several days. Chronic toxicity secondary to high-concentration exposure on a daily basis may also occur. Carbon monoxide's relationship to the production of coronary atherosclerosis remains debatable, perhaps less so in those concomitantly exposed to cigarette smoke and individuals exposed on a daily basis in specific occupations.[135,136] The exposure of firefighters to carbon monoxide poses less risk, as this is generally not on a daily, continual basis or in high concentrations because of protective external breathing devices.

Guidotti, after an extensive review of occupational mortality among firefighters concluded the following:[137]

1. There is no evidence of an increased risk of death from heart disease.
2. Sudden death, myocardial infarction, or fatal arrhythmia occurring on or soon after near maximal stress on the job are likely to be work-related.
3. "Heart attacks" occurring away from work cannot be presumed to be work-related.
4. Job-related sedentary lifestyle and personal risk factors (smoking, lipidemia, hypertension, diabetes, family history, etc.) are more reflective of an adverse health effect being involved in the causation of heart disease in these individuals, rather than any work-related involvement.
5. Some evidence from clinical studies suggests a risk of sudden cardiac decompensation and a risk of a heart attack with sudden maximal exertion and after exposure to CO, and suggests that this did not translate into an excess risk of fatal heart attack at a later date.
6. If a firefighter did have a heart attack during or within a day after a fire, it would be reasonable to call it a work-related event.

Glueck et al., concluded that firefighters who later developed coronary heart disease (CHD) and those without CHD did not differ by history of smoke inhalation.[138] They noted that cigarette smoking, hypertension, hyperlipidemia, and family history were more important risk factors than exposure to CO. Recent studies have indicated that up to 37% of patients following moderate to severe exposure to CO (poisoning) may sustain myocardial toxicity (injury) based on the elevation of cardiac enzymes and abnormal electrocardiograms. It was also concluded that short- and long- term mortality increased in this patient population. An investigative report by Kalay et al. studied 20 patients diagnosed as having CO poisoning and found that the extent of myocardial toxicity and dysfunction was dose- and time-related.[139] The degree of left ventricular dysfunction (ejection fraction) correlated with the level of carboxyhemoglobin on blood sampling. All patients had normal coronary angiograms. It was concluded that most of the myocardial dysfunction dissipates within 24 hours.

Particulate Air Pollution

The harmful effects of air pollution are finally becoming a recognized and highly important factor in the development of disease and in the aggravation of preexisting disease states. These include cancer, lung and heart disease, and other conditions that receive less attention. Particulate air pollution is a mixture of suspended solid and liquid particles of various sizes and compositions. These include various kinds of soot, carbon monoxide, sulfur dioxide, nitrogen dioxide, ozone, many types of volatile organic compounds and gasses, pollens, dusts, spores, and a host of harmful legal and illegal substances produced by various industries.[140]

The production and progression of atherosclerosis resulting from air pollution is now proven fact, experimentally and epidemiologically.[141,142,143] The subsequent effects of plaque production and rupture, coagulopathic and thrombotic effects, arterial vasoconstriction, systemic inflammatory response, and various neuro-humeral responses have been implicated in the production of angina pectoris, heart failure, and cardiac arrhythmia. These adverse effects can lead to myocardial infarction, a proclivity for enhanced artificial pacemaker activity, and sudden death.

The effects on the pulmonary system include acute and chronic bronchitis, pneumonitis, bronchial asthma, hypersensitivity syndrome, and lung cancer. Allergic rhinitis and dermatitis are also frequent accompaniments of particulate air pollution. Unbridled diesel fumes are one of the most hazardous producers of various disease states in today's world. This has been reviewed in more detail in the book *Your Car Can Be Hazardous To Your Health*.[144]

Radiation Therapy

The cardiovascular side effects and complications of radiation therapy are numerous, and are often not considered in a differential diagnosis of cardiac pathologic states (Table 15.7).

Table 15.7 Cardiovascular Effects of Radiation Therapy

Cellular damage
Vascular damage
Enhanced atherosclerotic occlusion
Pericarditis (acute and chronic)
Pericardial effusion
Constrictive pericarditis
Myocardial fibrosis
Conduction defects (ECG)
ST-T abnormalities (ECG)
Aggravation of heart failure

Occlusive coronary disease generally manifests itself 6 to 12 years following exposure. It is a distinct pathologic entity. In the presence of inherent coronary arterial occlusive disease, this timetable can occur much sooner when damage to preexisting coronary lesions appears likely.

The increasingly prevalent use of radiation therapy for mediastinal tumors, lung cancer, breast cancer, lymphomas, and so on has resulted in increased exposure of the heart to radiation-induced abnormalities and their associated pathophysiology. A case of ostial stenosis of the left main and right coronary arteries has been reported in a patient who received mediastinal radiation for Hodgkin's disease.[145] This patient received radiation therapy 21 years previously at the age of 23.

Hull et al. presented an excellent review of valvular dysfunction and carotid, subclavian, and coronary artery disease in patients who received radiation therapy for Hodgkin's lymphoma.[146] They found an incidence of coronary artery disease in 10.4% of those who were diagnosed at a median of 9 years posttherapy, carotid and/or subclavian disease at a median of 17 years posttherapy, and a 6.2% incidence of valvular dysfunction at a median of 22 years after treatment. The most common valvular affliction was aortic stenosis. Mitral stenosis, mitral insufficiency, tricuspid insufficiency, and aortic insufficiency were less commonly found.

Heidenreich et al.[147] studied 294 asymptomatic patients who received mediastinal radiation and found that a significant number of patients who presented without any cardiac symptoms were diagnosed as having aortic regurgitation, tricuspid regurgitation, aortic stenosis, and myocardial dysfunction or myocardial muscle mass loss. They recommended that these patients be considered for screening electrocardiography and echocardiography on a selective basis. Another group reported a combination of severe tricuspid insufficiency, moderate aortic insufficiency, restrictive cardiomyopathy, and constrictive pericarditis producing right-sided heart failure in a patient 30 years following mediastinal radiation for Hodgkin's disease.[148]

A review of cardiac morbidity from breast cancer treatments presented in the *Journal of Clinical Oncology* (Volume 24, 2006) noted the production of cardiac muscle dysfunction in 30% of patients receiving trastuzumab chemotherapy and the long-term risk for the production of coronary artery disease in breast cancer patients receiving radiation therapy.

Medication-Induced Cardiac Valvulopathy

Drugs known to cause valvular heart damage are **methysergide** and **ergotamine**, used for treatment of migraine headaches, **dexfenfluramine** and **fenfluramine**, previously used for weight reduction, and **pergolide**, currently used in the treatment of **Parkinson's disease**.

A report from the Mayo Clinic discusses three patients with **pergolide-induced severe tricuspid regurgitation**, accompanied by left-sided regurgitation in two patients.[149]

A major medical–legal catastrophe was created by the **"fen-phen" controversy**, which began in 1999. The majority of those involved in the class action lawsuits were nothing but "bandwagon jumpers." A significant number of cases were unjustified or unjustifiable. Many physicians declined to examine these patients as expert independent medical examiners, other than those rare patients in their own practices who were prescribed the drug by themselves or another physician, as the majority of physicians had never prescribed these drugs because of previously known side affects involving the possibility of causing pulmonary hypertension. Reports indicated that fen-phen was a causative factor in the production of valvular insufficiency (mitral and aortic) in 5 to 9% of patients with significant lesions and 12 to 16% with mild regurgitation.[150,151]

Investigators feel strongly that the incidence of valvulopathy in fen-phen users is dose and time dependent. It has also been noted that early or mild lesions may regress after discontinuation of the drug.[152,153] A report from the Mayo Clinic also indicated that valvular heart disease did not appear to progress after cessation of fen-phen use, and that the echocardiographic valvular features appeared to improve with time.[154] These conclusions were also supported by other studies that evaluated the natural history and progression of echocardiographially determined valvulopathy.[155,156]

Drug-Induced Electrocardiographic Changes

The number of drugs that are known to influence the ECG are legion, and would require a textbook on the subject. In a practical sense, almost any drug can affect the ECG. Effects can appear as cardiac arrhythmias, conduction disturbances, and alterations of depolarization (QRS) or repolarization (ST-T). Factors that predispose any given patient to various electrocardiographic abnormalities are metabolic and electrolyte imbalance (hypokalemia, hyperkalemia, hypomagnesemia, acidosis, hypocalcemia, hypoxemia), preexisting heart disease of any type, heart failure, renal failure, hepatic dysfunction, and genetically induced predispositions that are known to affect the QT interval.

Increasing attention in the medical literature is being paid to **prolongation of the QT interval** on the ECG. The number of drugs known to affect the QT interval keeps increasing and seems limitless. The primary concern is that patients who are known to have prolonged QT intervals or those unsuspected of having a predisposition to QT prolongation when given certain drugs can further prolong the QT interval, leading to ventricular tachycardia, ventricular fibrillation, and sudden death. These arrhythmogenic cardiotoxic effects can also occur in cases of **methadone overdose**, which prolongs the QT interval and results in ventricular tachycardia, ventricular fibrillation, and sudden death. A Danish study reported that syncope occurred in 32% of methadone users who had a QTc greater than 440 ms. A direct relationship to the daily dose and the QTc was noted. The patients given buprenorphine did not have an increase in the QT interval or suffer syncopal episodes. It is believed that torsade de pointes was the cause of syncope.

The long QT syndrome may be congenital or acquired. There are presently 10 identified basic genetic electrophysiologic subforms of the prolonged QT syndrome. These involve specific biochemical dysfunction of potassium, sodium, and calcium channels at a subcellular level. It is believed that additional defects may also have a role in this regard, and they have been classified beyond the three initially recognized and more commonly occurring types. These have been classified as QT 4, 5, 6, 7, 8, 9, and 10. QT prolongation predisposes individuals to the development of ventricular arrhythmia by prolonging myocardial repolarization, thereby causing undesirable "afterdepolarizations" with erratic dispersion of the myocyte refractory periods (an electrophysiologic disturbance).

Currently under investigation is a short QT syndrome (SQTS) with QT intervals of less than 300 to 320 ms. Similar to the long QT syndrome (LQTS), SQTS can lead to ventricular fibrillation, but in contrast, may present as atrial fibrillation. It also is known to be related to sudden death. Its association with and aggravation by various influences has not yet been categorically defined. Also in contrast to LQTS, SQTS may be alleviated by quinidine, which can be harmful in patients with LQTS, who are often treated with beta-blockers or calcium channel blockers. ICD placement for the secondary prevention of ventricular fibrillation is necessary and is usually dependent upon the family history, patient history, and clinical circumstances. Some investigators have advocated ICD placement for primary prevention as well. LQTS-1 commonly occurs on exertion, LQTS-2 may can be triggered by anxiety and emotional states, and LQTS-3 can occur during sleep. The effects of these extraneous influences on SQTS have not been notably defined.

The **gastrointestinal propulsive drug cisapride** and two second-generation antihistamines (astemizole and terfenidine) were removed from the market because of their propensity to cause torsade de pointes (TDP), a lethal ventricular dysrrhythmia. Drugs in the antibiotic class may also cause prolongation of the corrected QT interval (QTc) and terminate in TDP. Those more commonly reported were **erythromycin** and second-generation **fluoroquinolones**. In general, a QTc longer than 450 ms is of potential concern, and a QTc interval greater than 500 ms is a substrate for progression to ventricular tachyarrhythmias.

Drugs used in the treatment of psychotic disorders are likewise prone to produce prolongation of the QTc interval and must be used with caution—some classes more so than others. Most frequently listed are the **phenothiazine** and **tricyclic psychotherapeutic** agents. The antidepressant drug **fluoxetine** has been reported as causing QT prolongation.[157] A black-box warning regarding the propensity of the sedative/anti-emetic drug **droperidol** to cause QT prolongation was published in late 2001. The commonly used first-generation antihistamine, **diphenhydramine**, when overdosed, can produce prolongation of the QTc.[158]

Clindamycin-induced ventricular fibrillation due to long QT syndrome has been reported but is apparently quite infrequent.[159]

Much attention has been given to the commonly used antibiotic **erythromycin** in this regard. The potential for serious dysrhythmia is increased because of the large number of drugs that are metabolized by or inhibit the CYP3A hepatic enzyme system, thereby causing increased risk of malignant dysrhythmias when certain drugs are used in combination. The use of erythromycin should therefore be avoided when patients are taking antifungal agents, diltiazem, verapamil, and cimetidine, among others. In addition, if patients have any morbidly predisposing factors that may enhance the development of cardiac arrhythmia as noted previously, it would be best to avoid the use of erythromycin singularly and most certainly in combination with any other drug that is known to prolong the QT interval or is metabolized by the hepatic CYP3A system. Some authors recommend an ECG before beginning erythromycin and on its cessation of therapy to detect QT prolongation in predisposed individuals.

A single dose of IV erythromycin has been shown to prolong the QTc interval.[160] That report recommended that erythromycin should be administered as a slow infusion and that ECG monitoring should accompany its use in critically ill patients, in those with electrolyte disturbance, and in patients taking drugs that have similar cardiac effects. Orban et al.[161] reported a typical case of erythromycin-induced TDP leading to ventricular fibrillation, and Katapadi et al.[162] reported a similar case and literature review up to 1997. The manufacturer of the antischizophrenic drug **haloperidol** has recently issued a warning of its effect on prolonging the QT interval and the possibility of sudden death.

VI

Technical, Epidemiologic, Social and Philosophical Influences

The Electrocardiogram 16

The resting electrocardiogram (ECG, EKG) is an invaluable, inexpensive, and easily performed noninvasive test, which can often lead one to suspect an otherwise unexplained or unrelated pathologic or physiologic cardiovascular derangement. When it is entirely normal, it means only that it is either totally normal or the underlying disease state has not as yet altered the ECG. Diseases in various stages of development or advancement can result in any number of ECG abnormalities. These include rhythm disturbances, conduction abnormalities, pseudo-scar Q wave development, pathologic Q waves, and, most frequently, ST and T wave changes. Abnormalities of the ST segment and T wave can be seen as depression of the ST segments below the baseline (isoelectric zone), decreases in T wave voltage and obvious T wave negativity. It can be aptly stated that any change from normal should be a cause for suspicion and observation, and these changes always have meaning, depending on the mechanism of production as caused by the underlying pathophysiologic alterations of the ECG during or after its interpretation by somebody who is competent and experienced in such matters.[163]

Many errors are made because of inadequate interpretation of the ECG and its correlation with the clinical state of the patient. Fortunately, these errors usually produce little or no harm to the patient, but they can be a source of anxiety and depression and a needless economic burden. Occasionally, serious consequences may result from an incorrectly read ECG—errors of omission or inclusion. Many errors can be avoided by having an experienced electrocardiographer review all computer-derived ECG interpretations. The largest study of its type revealed that an overall correction of computer-derived ECG interpretations was necessary in 48% of cases.[164] It is therefore mandatory that an experienced electrocardiographer review computer-generated ECG interpretations in order to avoid inappropriate management decisions.

Errors can originate from several categories: technical, normal variants, physiologic influences, noncardiac pathologic conditions, and the numerous cardiac diseases that involve any anatomic cardiac structure. Technical errors can originate from the patient, the technician, the electrical line, or the equipment. Numerous physiologic influences can alter almost any portion of the ECG. The more common of these secondary influences are drugs (therapeutic and illicit), electrolyte imbalances, endocrine diseases, anemia, and renal failure. Less well known, but not uncommon, is the association of ECG abnormalities with acute abdominal conditions (pancreatitis, cholecystitis).[165,166]

Of more recent vintage has been the recognition of electrocardiographic changes associated with neurologic events.[167] These changes include deeply negative (ischemic type) T waves, tall (upright) T waves, changes in the QT interval, prominent U waves, conduction defects, and arrhythmias.[168] These changes are believed to be due to catecholamine excess, alterations in the calcium channels, influences on the beta-receptors, and other indeterminate effects secondary to cerebral stimulation.

In addition to the errors imparted by computer-generated ECG reports, one must maintain a sense of vigilance for the not uncommon false-positive and false-negative results, which can occur on either the resting ECG or poststress ECG. Usually, these must be verified by association with a scintographic scan (nuclear imaging) or echocardiography. Even then, the so-called verification may not be definitive or confirmatory, and a cardiac catheterization is necessary to assist in determining the final solution. This is especially important in the assessment of coronary arterial disease, usually atherosclerotic in origin.

In conclusion, the ECG can be a source of consternation for the physician as well as the patient. A conscientious, careful, knowledgeable, and experienced assessment and evaluation is necessary in order to avoid (as best as is possible) the side effects of misinterpretation and inadequate or incomplete evaluation, observation, and follow-up.

Stress

17

The definition of stress is elusive and often highly subjective. In medical-legal circles, psychological stress is for the most part an overplayed, unduly emphasized, highly misunderstood, misused, and mislabeled composition of opinions largely related to which side of the evaluation is being presented—defense or plaintiff, usually the latter. Some authorities have argued that use of the term should be discontinued. Nevertheless, stress is a valid concept from both the physical and psychological points of view. In legal and judicial matters, much emphasis and fallacious statements and interpretations are made in the name of *stress*.

None of the premiere textbooks of medicine and cardiology list stress as a risk factor for the development of cardiovascular disease. That is not to say that certain types of psychological stresses are not important and should be neglected. A qualitative and quantitative assessment is absolutely necessary, and is generally not obtained even in the best of studies; when done, it is based on highly subjective and limited objective data.

Overwhelming scientific data attributes an increased risk of cardiac morbidity and mortality are genetically induced factors, smoking, hypertension, diabetes, obesity, and physical inactivity. The genetically induced risk factors are abnormalities of lipid metabolism (total cholesterol, especially with high LDL and low HDL, lipoprotein (a), elevated triglycerides), elevated homocysteine levels, coagulopathic abnormalities that can affect platelet function and the clotting mechanism, and other factors that presently have not been fully elucidated. Small particle-sized LDL is now known to be a greater risk factor than large-sized LDL particles. Research is presently focused on HDL subtypes. Various studies have attempted to correlate psychosocial factors with cardiovascular disease or outcomes, but none are assuredly conclusive. This includes the so-called type A personality. That is not to say that anxiety, depression, hostility, and sudden severe emotional shock are not important or should be neglected, but they must be placed in a more rigid and scientifically engendered perspective. It should not be an emotionally contrived, inaccurate opinion or conclusion used to implicate the multitude of the common daily stresses to which everyone is subjected. These cannot be linked to the causation of cardiovascular events. Tennant et al. have shown that if one combines prospective studies with angiography, stressful life events are not associated with the production or acceleration of atherosclerosis.[169]

It has been known for decades that the extremely traumatic stress associated with the death of a family member or loved-one, causing severe bereavement, can be implicated in causing certain individuals to be at an increased risk for cardiovascular events.[170] This has also been noted for certain "natural" disasters such as earthquakes, fires, explosions, and floods.[171]

Intense **anger** has been related to the production of myocardial infarction in the subsequent two hours after an outburst.[172] Interestingly, those patients who were taking aspirin on a regular basis had approximately half the risk of developing an anger-related myocardial infarction. The overall incidence in the two-hour group was 2.4%. Hlatky et al., in a study of 1,489 patients, concluded that **job strain** was not correlated with the prevalence or severity of coronary artery disease in a cohort of patients who underwent coronary angiography, and the level of disease was not affected by the level of job strain.[173] The study was of added significance compared to its predecessors, not merely in concluding that job strain had no correlation with the prevalence or the severity of coronary artery disease, but because the study was adequately adjusted for confounding factors and strengthened by the association with coronary arterial angiographic analyses. The Honolulu Heart Study also found no relationship between occupational strain and the subsequent incidence of coronary artery disease in a prospective cohort study.[174]

A report presented at the conference on Cardiovascular Disease Epidemiology and Prevention sponsored by the American Heart Association (2001, San Antonio, Texas) concluded that smoking may trigger an acute myocardial infarction and that the thrombus area in the infarct-related artery (even in the absence of other risk factors) was considerably increased. The increased propensity toward the development of infarction occurred in those who smoked from less than 1 hour to 24 hours preceding the infarction, with the greatest incidence occurring from less than 1 hour to 6 hours before the event.

Environmental stress secondary to particulate air pollution has been linked to the progression of atherosclerosis and vulnerability to plaque rupture as well as an increased incidence of cardiac death.[143] This is just one of many biochemically induced stressors that can be related to pollution. Furthermore, it has been shown that elevated levels of particulate air pollution that are below the current EPA limits are associated with an increased rate of hospital admissions for exacerbation of congestive heart failure.[175] This is just one of many reasons for the absolute necessity of automobile ventilation filtration systems (micro-filters, dust and pollen filters, in-cabin air filters, under-hood filters, etc.) because of our polluted environment. Those that contain carbon or activated charcoal are preferable, as they help reduce the odor and fume content of the incoming air. Further helpful information on this subject can be obtained from Reference 144 and calling toll free 1-888-280-7715. The incidence of many health problems, especially those related to the cardiovascular and pulmonary systems, can be decreased or their severity diminished by adequate automobile ventilation filtration systems.

The following comments, opinions and conclusions have been derived or excerpted from the world medical literature. These reports are usually based predominantly upon epidemiologic studies, and some may border on being anecdotal in spite of various attempts at controls, adjustments for numerous confounding risk and other factors, and complicated statistical analyses. Some cannot be considered to be the ultimate or final word on the proposed subject of psychologic stress. They should be assessed as being imprecise observational data, which have uncertain or limited value compared to data with specific and more easily defined underlying pathophysiology.

- High degrees of chronic stress and brief bouts of acute stress increase the heart rate and blood pressure. These changes are more prominent in people who are highly reactive and are physically deconditioned, the latter enhancing decreased vagal tone.
- Depression is associated with an increased risk of death or myocardial infarction during the year after hospitalization for unstable angina.
- Hostile individuals were shown to have increased coronary artery calcification and therefore increased risk of coronary artery disease.
- Anger-prone individuals, even with normal blood pressure, appear to be at increased risk of cardiac events (myocardial infarction, arrhythmias) and recurrent cardiac events.
- Chronic stress may potentiate underlying situational heart disease, and acute stress may precipitate overt cardiac events.
- At the American Heart Association meeting in Dallas, Texas (Nov. 1986), Dr. Thomas Pearson (Johns Hopkins Hospital) stated that: "stress has become a meaningless catch word that fuels public overreaction, and that its ranking (as a culprit in heart disease) is undeserved."
- There is much controversy over the role that stress and personality play in the development of heart disease, as well as to what extent they may contribute to the progression of heart disease.
- Nationwide, stress-related workmen's compensation claims have risen dramatically and are an exceptionally formidable cause of employer fiscal problems, not only in settlement of exaggerated and unfounded claims, but in overall insurance costs and premiums. Some states do not allow stress claims unless they are unusual, unexpected, or extraordinary. Two stories of note on the absurdity of excesses of bureaucracy are the jogger in Hawaii who was allowed a compensable heart attack "because he was thinking about his job while jogging" and a state superior court judge whose widow was awarded a survivor's benefit on the "assumption that he had been overworked" and must have been mulling over his duties while he dropped dead picking strawberries on a Saturday afternoon.

- Some studies have disputed the relationship between mortality and coronary atherosclerosis and type A personality and have actually demonstrated greater mortality among type B patients.
- There exists the probability that continued levels of highly emotional stress over many months or years may play a role in the acceleration of coronary atherosclerosis. (But why has it not been shown as explicitly in peripheral vascular disease?)
- An isolated episode of severe emotional stress may precipitate a cardiovascular event in persons with coronary artery disease, especially when those individuals are physically unfit.
- Sudden cardiac death has been documented to occur from vigorous physical exertion above 6 METS (metabolic equivalents) in habitually sedentary individuals.
- The risk of exertion-related myocardial infarction is 50 times higher in less active individuals.
- The duration of increased risk following vigorous activity usually lasts less than 1 hour.
- The risk of myocardial infarction and sudden death occurs generally during the strenuous activity and persists most often for 15 to 30 minutes following the activity.

The latter four conclusions were based on an excellent review of triggers of acute cardiac events by Mittleman, who addressed his experience combined with a world literature review on the subject.[176]

- An isolated episode of acute, severe emotional stress can precipitate an acute cardiac event in certain susceptible individuals.
- Many workers actually have more personal, environmental, home, and social stressors than work-related stress.
- Physical inactivity and obesity are risk factors for the progression of cardiovascular disease.
- The physiologic and pharmacologic effects of excessive long-term stress are believed to contribute to the development and progression of cardiovascular disease. These effects are increases in abnormal lipids, increased lipolysis, coagulation system dysfunction, hypertension, increased cardiac output, increased heart rate, endothelial dysfunction, and secretion of cortisol, catecholamines, serotonin, and other products of the enzymatic and hormonal systems. The end result is a disturbance in blood clotting, lipid metabolism, blood viscosity, and cardiovascular dynamics.[177]
- Two hours of conditioning physical activity per week can reduce heart attack incidence by as much as 60% compared to sedentary status.
- There appears to be a correlation between atherosclerosis progression as demonstrated in the carotid arteries in association with exaggerated

blood pressure responses caused by mental stress that has been related to high job demands (low control and time pressure).

- Vigorous routine exercise lowers risk factors for coronary events more than moderate activity.
- Acute myocardial infarction and sudden cardiac deaths surge between 6 a.m. and noon.
- Emotional frustration and tensions are known to trigger silent myocardial ischemia.
- Hopelessness, defensiveness, anger, and depression have been limited to increased risk of adverse cardiac events.
- The risk of having a myocardial infarction goes up the day after the death of a loved one.
- The risk of mental-stress-induced ischemia is associated with significantly higher rates of subsequent fatal and nonfatal cardiac events.
- Mental stress during daily life (including feelings of sadness, frustration, and tension) can double the risk of myocardial ischemia within the next hour.
- A study reported in the *American Journal of Hypertension* concluded that stressful occupations are not linked to hypertension.
- Depression may be associated with an increased risk for coronary heart disease in men and women, as well as mortality in men, but not women.
- Hostile young adults are at an increased risk for the development of coronary artery disease.
- Mental stress has been shown to worsen the progression (in women) of coronary heart disease.
- Bereavement can trigger myocardial infarction in older women.
- The rate of cardiac arrhythmias doubled during the 30 days following the 9-11 disaster.
- Depression appeared to be an independent risk factor for the development and progression of coronary artery disease in men.
- Severe outbursts of anger or acute severe mental stress may trigger a cardiac event within 1 hour of the incident.
- Fatal myocardial infarction when attributed to stress occurs within 24 hours of the event.
- Myocardial infarction associated with stressful events generally occurs within 1 to 2 hours following the event.
- A study reported at the American College of Cardiology meeting in 1992 by Gambrielle and colleagues concluded that mental stress was an uncommon trigger of myocardial ischemia during daily life activities in medically treated patients with severe coronary artery disease.

- Severe psychosocial stress has been associated with an approximate twofold increase in stroke events in the presence of recent severe adverse life events or constant long-term stress.[178]

A brief review of **acute myocardial infarction triggered by emotional stress** concluded that most victims of stress-induced myocardial infarction were reported to have significant psychologic stress within 24 hours before death, often within 30 minutes.[179] An excellent review by Macleod et al., concluded that the data suggesting an association between psychologic stress and cardiovascular disease outcomes often leads to a spurious association between the two.[180]

The association of **physical stress and acute myocardial infarction** is at times equally ambiguous. More often than not, it is actually erroneous as a medical conclusion. Medical, legal, and judicial opinion is likewise generally erroneous with regard to the erratic opinions concerning shear stress. Shear stress is a necessary and important complement to vascular health and stability.[181,182,183] Normal and increased hemodynamic shear stress is vascularly protective. It is those areas where shear stress is diminished and blood flow is more erratic that are predisposed to atherosclerosis. These areas are typically located at the outer edges of vessel bifurcations. Increased shear stress in any other area of an artery enhances endothelial function and vasodilatation provided that the artery is undamaged by atherosclerosis, plaque, or thrombus. These pathologic changes are caused by various risk factors: smoking, hypertension, diabetes, hyperlipidemia, coagulopathic disorders, infectious and inflammatory processes, and other genetically predisposed conditions. Wherever blood flow exhibits stasis or direction reversal and shear is of diminished magnitude, the association with atheroscleratic plaque formation is enhanced.

A study involving 1,228 patients following an acute myocardial infarction revealed that 4.4% reported heavy physical exertion within one hour prior to onset.[184] Physical exertion is protective when performed regularly, and has been known to decrease the risk of cardiovascular events, but sudden or continued excessively heavy exertion can trigger acute cardiovascular events and myocardial infarction in sedentary individuals who have coronary or cardiac pathology. The believed mechanism is plaque rupture in response to hemodynamic stress, the outcome being dependent upon thrombus formation and vasoconstriction. The study concluded that heavy physical exertion could be identified as a trigger of myocardial infarction in only 3.8% of cases.

The risk of myocardial infarction associated with strenuous physical activity usually occurs during the activity or within one hour following the exertion.[185] There is an increased incidence of acute myocardial events in patients with known or undiagnosed coronary artery disease in the early morning hours, either during sleep or after awakening and engaging in routine activities. This is believed to be associated with the circadian increases in blood pressure, heart rate, and platelet aggregation as well as a decrease in fibrinolytic activity.[186] It is accepted that acute myocardial infarction can be precipitated by manual or machine-related snow removal. This generally occurs in habitually sedentary persons with risk factors for coronary artery disease (high blood pressure, abnormal lipid elevations, previous and present smoking, obesity, and diabetes) in whom a known or unknown diagnosis of coronary artery disease is present.[187]

Exertion-related angina pectoris is a common presentation of coronary artery disease, often presenting as the first sign or symptom. These patients are in contrast to those whose first sign or symptom is that of an acute myocardial infarction, approximately half of which will result in sudden death. It is generally accepted that regular moderate to vigorous physical activity and exercise is protective against sudden death.[188] Individuals not conditioned to physical activity are more likely to experience sudden death, as are those who have known or unknown coronary artery disease. It has been estimated that the risk of sudden death during vigorous exertion is exceptionally low (1 per 1.51 million episodes).[188,189,190] The highest frequencies of exertional sudden death occur during or shortly after (within 1 hour) the implicated activity.

It has been estimated that from 6 to 17% of all sudden deaths are associated with exertion. The implicated activity is usually of a type that those afflicted are unaccustomed to or greater than they are accustomed to performing. The overall risk of sudden death was not found to be increased by increased frequency of vigorous exercise. The Framingham Study found no relationship between physical activity and sudden death during a 20-year followup.[191]

A study comparing the clinical and angiographic characteristics of exertion-related acute myocardial infarction to nonexertional infarction revealed that the following were more frequently found in the exertional group: increased incidence in men, hyperlipidemia, smoking history, and presentation with ventricular fribrillation.[192] Also noted was an increased incidence of heart failure, single-vessel coronary disease, a large thrombus in the infarct-related artery, and low activity status. Those individuals most prone to sudden death caused by exertion are persons with severe coronary artery disease in whom associated plaque rupture was found (68%) compared to those dying at rest (23%).[193]

In conclusion, the following opinions are justified regarding the present status of psychosocial, environmental, and physical stressors on their relationship to cardiovascular disease and its associated events.

The statement attributed to Dr. Pearson made two decades ago at the American Heart Association in Dallas, Texas, is still valid today: "Stress has become a meaningless catchword that fuels public over-reaction. Its ranking (as a culprit in heart disease) is not deserved by the scientific evidence available." Studies to date are predominantly those of a highly statistically encumbered epidemiologic nature. Their structure, methods, and opinions are open to conjecture, question, and criticism. The previously accepted association and importance of type A and B personalities with reference to cardiovascular disease has recently come under considerable question and debate.

It is usually the spontaneous nature of plaque fissuring and rupture that is involved in the process and production of acute cardiac events, and only a lesser (albeit unknown) percentage of cardiac events are proven to be due to exertional or psychosocial stressors. These processes occur in arteries involved in the atherogenic process as influenced mainly by genetically induced factors and comorbid disease states.

Once the pathophysiologic process begins, it tends to be self-perpetuating in these individuals. It then secondarily triggers other concomitant physiologic changes involving endothelial function, clotting mechanisms, inflammation, and thrombosis. The usual physiologic responses to ordinary stressful events that are called into play during daily life are generally brief and not harmful. It has been postulated that they are necessary and beneficial. Physical stress is certainly more definable as a rule, and can often be quantified in contrast to the highly subjective nature of psychological stress. The individual perception of physical and psychological stress is highly variable and is greatly influenced by individual (subjective) perception. It is the persistence of intense, continued stress, whether physical or emotional that present research on the subject requires focusing. Stress-related activity is more definable in terms of physical stress as relegated to those habitually inactive individuals and those already afflicted (known or unknown) with coronary heart disease.

Psychosocial stress is not quantifiable or qualitatively precise in terms of its definition. Much data on the influence of emotional stress has come from animal experiments that are not necessarily transferable to everyday human situations. Similarly, the social and demographic data usually obtained in epidemiologic studies and analyses fail to definitively prove a relationship between occupational factors and cardiovascular disease and events except as indicated by very specific exposures and occupational circumstances. The production of anginal chest pain, cardiac arrhythmias, and myocardial infarction due to various stressors is not a point of disagreement, it is merely the application of the pathophysiologic principles involved that must be properly ascertained and placed into proper perspective. We can conclude that presently, the precise role of psychosocial stress in the development of cardiovascular disease and subsequent events is open to question, possesses great variability, and is subject to considerable uncertainty and controversy.

Illustrative Case Reports

VII

Case Reports 18

Case 1: Blunt Chest Trauma Resulting in Traumatic Tricuspid Insufficiency[194]

A 24-year-old male was seen in the emergency room following an accident during which his car hit a building. He sustained steering-wheel chest trauma, facial lacerations, a mediastinal hematoma, hematoma of the left lower lung, subdural hematoma, two rib fractures, and a right ankle fracture. A grade 2/6, soft, high-pitched, blowing, pansystolic murmur was present at the lower left sternal border. The heart rate was 130 per minute, and a third heart sound was noted. Cardiac enzymes CK-MB and troponin I levels were markedly elevated and were compatible with myocardial injury. The ECG one month following the accident (Figure 18.1) revealed a right axis shift, severe poor R-wave progression from leads V1 through V6, and an inferolateral repolarization abnormality not previously present. Cardiac catheterization was performed four months postaccident because of increasing dyspnea and a feeling of chest pressure. Operative evaluation of the heart revealed a markedly enlarged right atrium and a dilated right ventricle and a circumferential tear in the anterior leaflet of the tricuspid valve, with the base of the papillary muscle completely torn from its attachment to the wall of the right ventricle. Surgical repair consisted of a pericardial patch to the anterior tricuspid leaflet, reinsertion of the papillary muscle to the wall of the right ventricle, and placement of an annular ring. The hospital course was uneventful, and the postdischarge course subsequently led to a completely normal lifestyle.

Forensic Implications

In this case, close postdischarge follow-up was appropriate, with readmission for surgery based on ECG changes, echocardiography, and symptoms, which led to cardiac catheterization and the expectant surgery. Certainly, the surgery could have been performed sooner, but as such, did not lead to permanent cardiac disability or death as has been seen in other cases of this type. Much of the trauma sustained during the accident could have been avoided had the patient worn his seatbelt. The accident itself could have been avoided if the patient was not intoxicated from alcohol. Fortunately, no innocent victims were involved as is often the case in the increasing numbers of accidents of this type in our

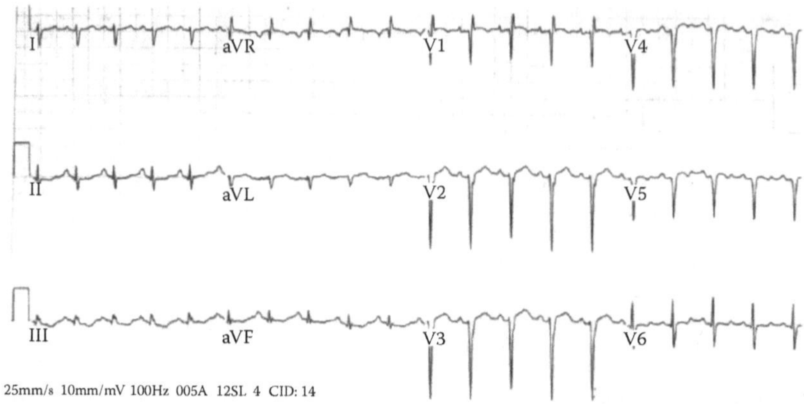

Figure 18.1 ECG one month post-accident. (RuDusky, B.M., Cimochowski, G., Traumatic tricuspid insufficiency- a case report. *Angiology*, 53:229–233, 2002. Reprinted with permission, SAGE Publications.)

present alcohol and drug-influenced society. Watchful waiting with close clinical observation following surgery was fortunate, but it must be remembered that sudden death could have intervened in association with heart failure and/or cardiac arrhythmia during the so-called recuperation period. This would have led to a plaintiff-favored verdict, as most situations of this magnitude are surgically corrected much earlier than four months postaccident. A six-week delay to allow healing of the associated myocardial and pulmonary contusions would have been a more logical approach, but even that delay can be catastrophic. The one-month postaccident ECG and echocardiogram were indicative of the severity of a situation requiring early intervention.

Case 2: Myocardial Contusion, Cardiac Rupture, and Sudden Death

A 17-year-old male was taken to the emergency room following a motor vehicle accident during which his vehicle hit a tree. He admitted to not wearing a seat belt. He complained of frontal head pain, knee and ankle pain, and central chest pain on inspiration. Physical examination revealed sternal ecchymosis and was otherwise negative. Laboratory tests revealed a hemoglobin of 12.0 g/dl and a white blood count of 13,200 K/μl. The chemistry profile, urinalysis, and chest x-ray were negative. Cardiac enzymes were not performed. A single preadmission ECG revealed normal sinus rhythm, negative T-wave in lead AVL and V-l, high takeoff of the ST segments in leads V1 and V2, and a biphasic T-wave in lead V2 (Figure 18.2). A repeat ECG was not done. The patient was admitted to orthopedic service for suturing of his knee and forehead lacerations and discharged the following morning. Two days later, the visiting nurse noted bilateral basilar rales. The patient complained of weakness, nausea, and light-headedness. Twenty-four days following hospital discharge he collapsed and could not be resuscitated.

The autopsy revealed 600 cc of blood in the pericardial sac due to a ruptured pseudoaneurysm of the anterior left ventricle, obviously causing pericardial tamponade (Figure 18.3).

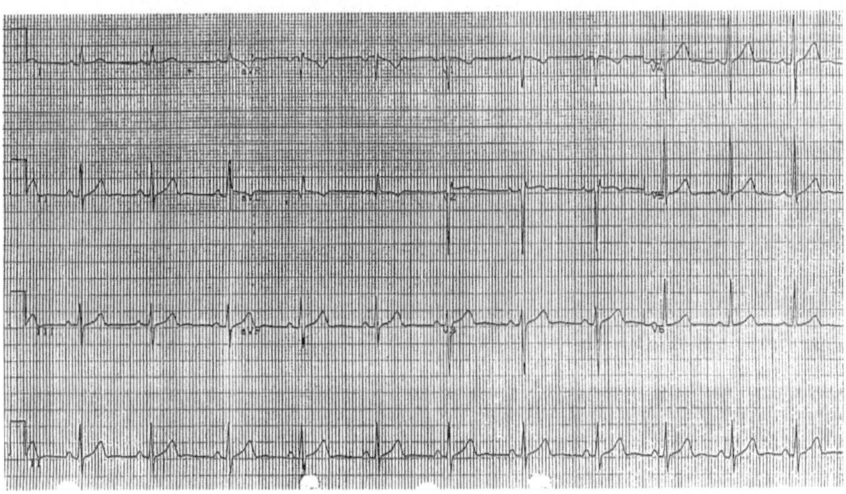

Figure 18.2 ECG post-accident revealing small q and negative T in AVL, negative T in V_1, and biphasically negative T in V_2, with high takeoff of the ST segment. (RuDusky, B.M., Myocardial contusion culminating in a ruptured pseudoaneurysm of the left ventricle. *Angiology,* 54:359–362, 2003. Reproduced with permission, SAGE Publications.)

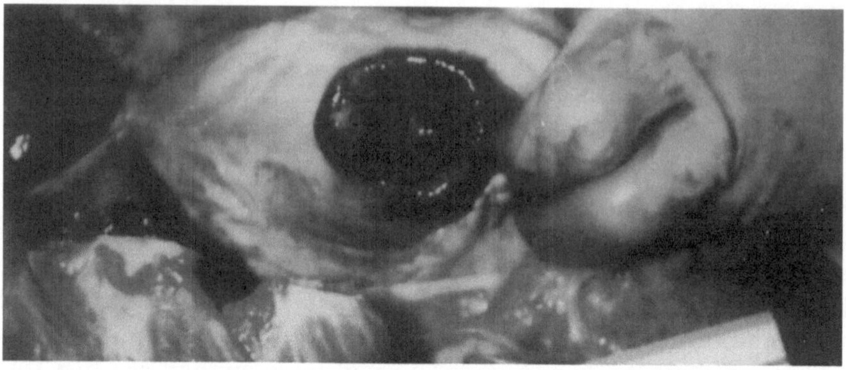

Figure 18.3 Autopsy revealing resected pericardium and ruptured pseudoaneurysm of the left ventricle. (RuDusky, B.M., Myocardial contusion culminating in a ruptured pseudoaneurysm of the left ventricle. *Angiology,* 54:359–362, 2003. Reproduced with permission, SAGE Publications.)

Forensic Implications

This case represented several causes of neglect: failure to consider a slightly decreased hemoglobin and increased white blood cell count, failure to consider suspicious ECG abnormalities, and not obtaining a repeat ECG prior to discharge. There was failure to properly evaluate, recognize, and observe a patient who had a high probability of having a myocardial contusion. Preadmission emergency room care was inappropriate and inadequate, as were admission and postdischarge care. The case was a guaranteed verdict for the plaintiff and was settled out of court for a very large monetary sum.

Case 3: Acute Myocardial Infarction in the Very Young[195,196]

The incidence of myocardial infarction in men between ages 14 to 35 years is approximately 1%, and in those younger than age 14 it is estimated at being less than 0.5%. Risk factors for its development are use of cocaine, trauma, tumors, various infections and inflammatory processes, familial hyperlipidemia, homocysteine excess, and certain genetic metabolic disorders.

A 16-year-old white male presented to the emergency room after waking up with acute onset precordial chest pain. The physical examination and basic laboratory studies, including a homocysteine level, were normal. The cardiac enzyme CK-MB and troponin I levels were markedly elevated. He was given thrombolytic therapy and supplementary low–molecular-weight heparin, aspirin, and beta-blockade. The ECG revealed evidence of an acute inferior myocardial infarction (Figure 18.4). Emergency cardiac catheterization revealed inferior wall hypokinesia and no obstructive disease, coronary or valvular. The hospital course was uneventful and uncomplicated. Studies

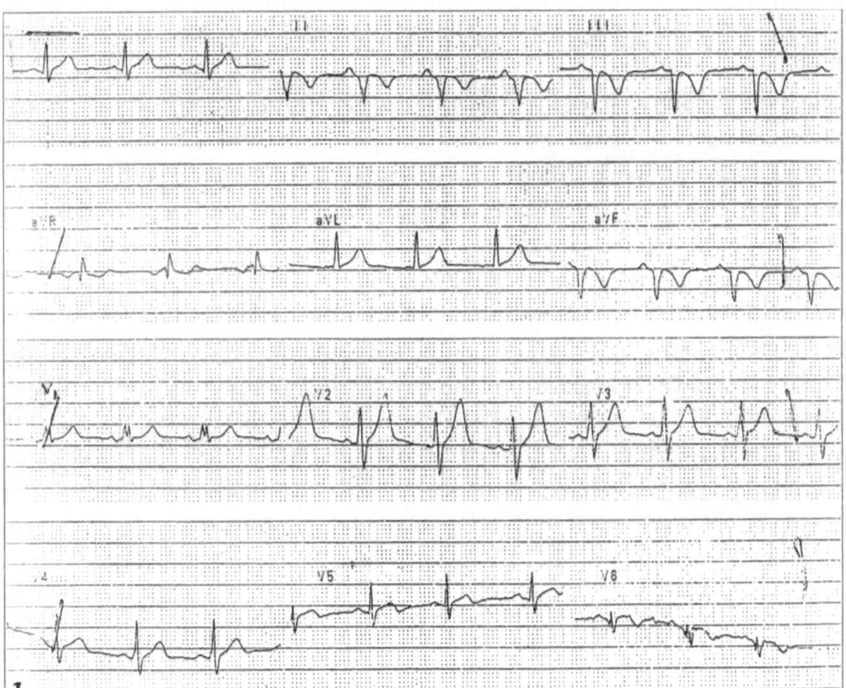

Figure 18.4 ECG on discharge, revealing inferolateral-apical infarction in a resolving state of evolution. (RuDusky, B.M., Lohin, D.L., Acute myocardial infarction in a 16-year-old male. *Angiology*, 54, 2003. Reprinted with permission, SAGE Publications.)

for lupus anticoagulant, activated protein C resistance, protein C activity, protein S activity, antithrombin III activity, and anticardiolipin antibodies were normal. The lipid profile was beyond the excellent level.

Forensic Implications

Similar cases reported in the medical literature in individuals from ages 14 to 22 years are obviously quite rare. The medical care and subsequent laboratory studies in this case and continued observation were excellent, as was the postdischarge follow-up.

In patients suffering acute myocardial infarction at a young age, thorough investigation is mandatory whether the coronary arteries are normal or abnormal. A detailed history in this case was entirely negative, with special emphasis on cigarette and pharmacologic drug use, as well as cocaine and other illicit drugs. Various factors that may affect cardiovascular function and produce disease (as noted in Table 18.1) were not present. There was a nondetailed and somewhat vague history of the patient having an emotional altercation with a parent that evening, the significance of which could not be determined. In these uncommon situations of acute myocardial infarction in young persons, the mechanism of causation is believed to be coronary vasospasm in the absence of overt disease states and risk factors. Speculation as to the possibility of coronary spasm incited by intense neruo-humoral physiologic mechanisms cannot be easily dismissed. These include events related to the production of intense sympathomimetic secretion, cortisol production, coagulopathic responses, and endothelial dysfunction.

Obviously, there were no positive forensic implications in this case. It was not influenced by employment, social entanglement, or sport activities. The diagnosis was immediately made, and appropriate emergency medical and diagnostic measures were undertaken. Subsequent studies to rule out underlying risk factors were performed. If these studies were not done, and recurrent myocardial infarction had occurred that could have created a state of complete disability or the death of the patient, medical-legal proceedings regarding malpractice are certain to have been instituted.

Table 18.1 Conditions that can Produce Coronary Arterial or Myocardial Disease

Inflammatory
Takayasu's arteritis
Rheumatic fever
Rheumatoid arthritis
Lupus erythematosus
Polyarteritis nodosa
Giant cell arteritis
Progressive systemic sclerosis
Kawasaki syndrome
Allergic reactions
Chemical toxins
Infectious diseases
Bacterial
Viral
Spirochetal
Fungal
Parasitic
Infiltrative and metabolic disorders
Hyperlipidemia
Hypothyroidism
Sarcoidosis
Neoplasms (primary, secondary)
Amyloidosis
Congenital and genetically induced metabolic disorders
Miscellaneous
Contraceptive drugs
Cocaine
Congenital anomalies of the coronary system
Cigarette smoking
Idiopathic coronary calcification and fibroplasias
Coronary vasospasm
Small-vessel coronary dysfunction
Myocardial contusion
Radiation therapy
Pharmacologic agents
Thromboembolic phenomena

Source: From: RuDusky, B.M., Lohin, D.H. *Angiology*, 54:106, 2003. With permission, SAGE Publications.

Case 4: Nitrate Holiday[198]

A young male was admitted to the hospital with severe chest pain of several hours duration. He worked in a munitions and explosive manufacturing plant as a shoveler and gel-stuffer, not always wearing his long gloves and respiratory mask. Several months previously he was admitted to the hospital with chest pain on a Monday morning. A treadmill stress test and cardiac catheterization were negative. He was a one pack per day cigarette smoker for many years. Again on an early Monday morning he sustained his second bout of chest pain, more severe than the initial episode. The ECG revealed minimal inferolateral ST-T changes and small q-waves in the inferior leads that were not previously present. An immediate cardiac catheterization revealed an 80% proximal right coronary artery narrowing that decreased to 10% following administration of intracoronary nitroglycerin. The hospital stay was uneventful, as was the postdischarge medical status. The invasive cardiologist believed that intense coronary vasospasm in an area of an insignificant atheroma was produced because of the enhanced sympathetic tone that occurred during the weekend withdrawal phase of his industrial nitroglycerin exposure.

Forensic Implications

The pathophysiologic effects of sustained exposure to organic nitrates, as well as its complications, are variously described in the medical literature.[197] These include hypotension, headache, tachycardia, and decreased venous return. Individual adaptation may produce diastolic hypertension, weakness, persistent sinus tachycardia, and, on occasion, cardiac arrhythmia. These side effects may take place after several weeks or months following exposure. Special clothing, respirator masks, and gloves are now being utilized in explosives manufacturing centers in order to prevent the cardiovascular effects and consequences of nitrate exposure.

This case was settled for a lump sum workmen's compensation payment. The claimant quit his job in the munitions manufacturing industry, obtained work elsewhere, and had no further cardiovascular complaints or problems.

Case 5: Thoracic Aortic Aneurysm

A middle-aged female presented for an independent medical examination (IME) for evaluation of a claimed aortic aneurysm following a motor vehicle accident (MVA) in which she was a seat-belted passenger, hit from behind by another automobile.

The history noted that a St. Jude aortic valve prosthesis was placed 13 years prior to the accident because of a severely stenosed bicuspid aortic valve. Additional diagnoses were hypertension and chronic obstructive pulmonary disease secondary to cigarette smoking. Three weeks following the accident the patient was hospitalized for chest, neck, and arm pain diagnosed as a whiplash injury with radiculopathy. A CT scan of the chest revealed a 5.6-cm fusiform dilation of the ascending aorta with no evidence of tear or dissection. A cardiac catheterization revealed an aneurysmal dilatation of the ascending aorta, normal valve function, and normal coronary arteries. Surgical intervention was advised, and an ascending aortic graft procedure was performed.

Forensic Implications

The patient claimed that the aortic aneurysm was due to the automobile accident. Clearly, it was not. The patient's aortic aneurysm dilatation was due to the natural preoperative progression often seen in cases of bicuspid aortic valve stenosis. It can also occur in a slowly progressive manner following placement of an aortic valve prosthesis years later. In addition, atherosclerotic vascular disease and genetically predisposed medial (elastic, collagen) degenerative changes are often found on pathologic examination.

The diffuse, fusiform nature of the aneurysm speaks against its occurrence as a result of the motor vehicle accident, as no dissection, tear, or rupture had taken place. The pathologic examination confirmed the opinions of the cardiovascular forensic specialist, and no economic or liability penalties were awarded to the plaintiff.

Case 6: Total Aortic Dissection

A 65-year-old male professional was admitted to the emergency room in extremus. He was screaming, restless, and had to be restrained, but was unresponsive to questions; his speech was unintelligible. Respiratory stridor with marked wheezing (inspiratory and expiratory) was present. The family noted that the patient had a long-standing history of bronchial asthma and had been on prednisone therapy for many years.

Physical examination revealed sinus tachycardia (115/min), blood pressure 168/68 mm Hg, diminished heart tones, a weak right carotid pulse, and a faint (grade 1/6), short, high-pitched diastolic murmur over the aortic area. Initial chest x-ray was unremarkable except for hyperinflation of the lungs. Laboratory studies revealed a hemoglobin of 11.2 gm/dl, white blood cell count of 12,100/μl, normal basic metabolic panel, and slight elevation of cardiac enzymes. The ECG revealed sinus tachycardia and elevated ST segments in the inferior leads, with negative T-waves. The patient was transferred to the intensive care unit and seen by the critical care internist, who recommended fibrinolytic therapy for an acute myocardial infarction. The cardiologist refused the order, requesting a repeat portable chest x-ray, now showing a slightly widened mediastinal shadow. An emergency CT scan was ordered and was positive for a dissection of the thoracic aorta in its entirety, the abdominal scan revealing dissection and continued false lumen of the entire abdominal aorta and iliac arteries. The patient was now comatose and had a flaccid left arm and leg with mottling of both legs. A cardiovascular surgeon was consulted, but the patient expired before being seen.

Forensic Implications

Awareness and astute consideration are necessary and often delayed in the diagnosis of dissecting aortic aneurysms. They can mimic numerous medical and surgical conditions affecting the thorax, chest, and abdomen. Aortic dissection is one of six diagnoses for which attending and consulting physicians must be constantly vigilant—acute myocardial infarction, pulmonary embolism, aortic dissection, pericardial tamponade, acute mesenteric ischemia, and heparin-induced thrombocytopenia (HIT). All six can be easily overlooked or misdiagnosed and can result in significant medical–legal consequences. It was fortunate that the attending cardiologist refused to follow the internist's recommendation for the administration of thrombolytic therapy. It was opined by three consultants that no medical or surgical measures would be of value in this patient. If, however, thrombolytic therapy or any other form of anticoagulation had been given, the severity and the consequences of the dissection could have erroneously been attributed to their use. Anticoagulation therapy is contraindicated in acute aortic dissection, just as it is in acute pericarditis or cardiac tamponade.

This patient suffered a heart attack and stroke simultaneously. Postmortem examination revealed obstruction of the right coronary artery, dehiscence of a portion of the aortic valve, obstruction of the carotid arteries, and varying degrees of involvement in all the branch arteries, one renal vein, and partial but significant occlusion of both iliac arteries. It was felt that long-term use of prednisone played a role in the production of the aortic degenerative changes and allowed a simple tear to proceed to a state of rapid and total dissection.

Case 7: Abdominal Aortic Aneurysm, Dissection, and Rupture

A 70-year-old male businessman requested a "complete checkup." He had a previous history of heavy alcohol consumption and cigarette smoking, both discontinued for approximately one year. The clinical examination revealed the presence of chronic obstructive pulmonary disease (emphysema), mild hypertension (143/94 mm Hg), a palpable pulsatile lower abdominal mass, and a faint infraumbilical systolic bruit. Laboratory studies were compatible with slight elevations of the liver enzymes secondary to fatty liver and/or inflammatory hepatic degeneration due to many years of alcohol ingestion. CT scan of the abdomen revealed an infrarenal abdominal aortic aneurysm of 5.1 cm diameter with mural thrombus formation and a false lumen. The patient was promptly referred to a vascular surgeon but chose to go on vacation for two weeks rather than keep the appointment. On returning from his trip, while getting off the plane, he developed sudden abdominal pain and collapsed. An ambulance was summoned, and the operating room notified. The admitting hemoglobin was 8.8 gm/dl. Intravenous fluids and packed red blood cells were started. An aortic bilateral iliac graft was placed. Postoperatively, the patient was noted to have a significant cognitive defect and no other complications.

Forensic Implications

The attending physician documented quite well the instructions given to the patient prior to confirming the diagnosis by CT scan. The patient was warned to do no exertive effort and not to play golf. He was also told that leaving for a vacation was unwise and could be dangerous. He was given a prescription for atenolol (a beta-blocker) to be started immediately. Depending on clinical circumstances, abdominal aortic aneurysms that are asymptomatic require attention for possible intervention when approaching 5.5 cm diameter. If discovered at smaller diameters (less than 5.0 cm), knowing the initial size and rate of enlargement is helpful in decision-making. This often remains unknown to attending and consulting physicians except when studies are done earlier for another reason. This patient "played the game" by his own rules and lost. It could not be determined as to whether the patient would have had prompt surgical intervention in order to prevent rupture of the aneurysm. If intervention was logistically delayed, the outcome in all probability would have been similar, vacation or not. Fortunately, the clinician was easily able to make and confirm the diagnosis and approached the problem excellently from all aspects.

Any alternative handling of the situation could have been medical-legally problematic—failure to diagnose, failure to treat, failure to inform, failure to restrict, and failure to consult. In this case all, were appropriately and systematically performed. It is important that attending physicians and consultants be aware that if medical and observational care is chosen for large aneurysms, for certain and specific reasons, disseminated intravascular coagulation (DIC) has been rarely known to occur. This can be a fatal or extremely morbid consequence. It is believed to be due to an over utilization of clotting factors in order to produce thrombosis over a large area of dysfunctional endothelium.

Case 8: Temporal Arteritis

A 75-year-old female was admitted to the hospital with a history of headache, slight fever, neck pain, and stiffness of several days' duration. The patient's history indicated a diagnosis of rheumatic heart disease with mitral insufficiency and aortic stenosis resulting in atrial fibrillation. A recent exposure to mosquito bites was noted. She was on warfarin anticoagulation as antithromboembolic prophylaxis for atrial fribrillation. Shortly after admission she complained of bilateral jaw pain. Physical examination was unremarkable except for the mitral and aortic systolic murmurs and slight stiffness of the neck. Interestingly, there was no significant tenderness to palpation of the temporal areas or palpable cords over the temporal arteries. Her preadmission medical treatment program consisted of digoxin, lasix, potassium chloride, warfarin, and low-dose aspirin.

Laboratory data revealed a normal complete blood count, sedimentation rate of 79 mm/hour and a normal chemistry profile. Screening studies for antinuclear antibodies, Lyme disease, West Nile virus, mononucleosis, and cryptococcal agglutinins were negative, as were blood and urine cultures.

A vascular surgery consult was requested for a temporal artery biopsy. The pathologist reported that it was the severest case of temporal arteritis he had pathologically diagnosed and was likewise amazed at the paucity of symptoms, especially the lack of visual symptoms or blindness. The patient was maintained on a lower dose of warfarin and placed on oral prednisone, beginning at 60 mg per day. After 6 weeks, the dosage was reduced slowly and successively every month and was discontinued at the end of the seventh month.

No complications occurred from the patient's disease or its treatment. Her warfarin-induced anticoagulation was increased to its original level, and she subsequently underwent open-heart surgery for replacement of her mitral valve and a tricuspid ring, with no consequences. A myocardial biopsy taken during surgery was negative for evidence of myocarditis.

Forensic Implications

Temporal arteritis when undiagnosed is a not uncommon cause of loss of vision. It may be accompanied by diffuse systemic manifestations involving a number of organ systems due to a diffuse vasculitis. Therapy under the best of circumstances is not always as successful as in this case, and the earlier the diagnosis and treatment, the better the chance of a successful outcome. Prompt diagnosis in spite of advanced disease not only prevented serious complications but resulted in a complete cure. Failure to diagnose and failure to treat would have led to disastrous medical–legal consequences.

Case 9: Disseminated Intravascular Coagulation and Heparin-Induced Thrombocytopenia

A 74-year-old female with a known history of mitral prolapse was admitted to the hospital with dyspnea and atrial tachycardia. Prior medical therapy included propranolol LA 60 mg for recurrent supraventricular tachycardia, fosinopril 10 mg daily for hypertension, and atorvastatin 10 mg for hyperlipidemia.

The patient reverted to normal sinus rhythm and a lesser stage of cardiac decompensation on a combination of digoxin, furosemide, potassium chloride, and a brief course of oral quinidine. Cardiac catheterization was performed and revealed normal coronary arteries and severe mitral regurgitation due to valvular disruption secondary to marked myxoid degeneration of both valve leaflets. Five days after a cardiac catheterization she underwent cardiac surgery, which resulted in placement of a St. Jude prosthetic mitral valve. Following surgery the patient developed ventricular fibrillation and postoperative bleeding originating from the right superior pulmonary vein. Bleeding continued and resulted in re-operation on the second and the third postoperative days. The surgeons noted superior vena caval thrombosis and performed an innominate vein to right atrium bypass, and during the fourth surgery a small laceration in the epicardium of the left ventricle was repaired and an aortic balloon pump was inserted. During a "stormy" 10-day period the patient sustained bilateral cerebellar and occipital strokes, a brain stem stroke accompanied by cerebral edema, and superior uncus herniation, the immediate cause of her demise.

The cardiologist, hematologist, and cardiac surgeon all realized the complexity, severity, and diagnostic laboratory problems with which this patient presented. Heparin was discontinued 4 days prior to her demise and was given because of the initial primary diagnosis of disseminated intravascular coagulation triggered by hemorrhage and shock. Enoxaparin was then begun subcutaneously every 12 hours, and transfusions of fresh frozen plasma were discontinued. The following factors were decreased: platelets, free and total protein S, antithrombin III, and fibrinogen. The prothrombin time, partial thromboplastin time, and fibrin degradation products were increased. Protein C, ristocetin cofactor, Von Willebrand antigen, D-dimer, factor VIII, and lupus screen were normal or negative. Heparin-induced antibody was positive on initial and repeat study. The D-dimer assay became positive. Platelet antigen and activation assays were not performed. The lowest platelet count was 27,000.

The following facts must be considered in the evaluation of a case of this complexity.

1. Platelets can be decreased significantly in DIC, HIT, and active thrombosis.
2. Protein C and protein S deficiency can occur in DIC or thrombotic states. In active thrombosis the depletion of specific proteins can lead

to an erroneous diagnosis of antithrombin, protein C, or protein S deficiency.

3. Heparin-induced antibodies can occur in non-HIT heparin-exposed patients.
4. The prothrombin and partial thromboplastin times can be increased by heparin or in patients with DIC.
5. Fibrinogen levels are usually decreased in DIC.
6. Increased fibrin degradation products occurs in DIC.
7. Antithrombin III is decreased by heparin and DIC.
8. D-dimer is increased during active thrombosis and DIC.
9. Warfarin anticoagulation can increase antithrombin III levels and decrease those of protein C and protein S, thereby leading to a misdiagnosis of inherited deficiency of these factors. Testing for these factors should therefore be withheld for two or more weeks after stopping warfarin.

The patient was seen by two hematologists, a cardiologist, and two cardiac surgeons. Disagreement ensued over the basic underlying causes of the hemorrhage and thromboses. It was ultimately decided that the patient suffered from both coagulopathic states—disseminated intravascular coagulation and heparin-induced thrombocytopenia. This is an uncommonly reported situation in the medical literature.

Forensic Implication

Since the advent and increasing use of heparin anticoagulation, the recognition and appropriate management of HIT has become extremely important, as litigation has become more frequent in these cases. Heparin-induced thrombocytopenia type II, can be considered to be the sixth imperative diagnosis that must be made by the attending or consulting physicians. The first five previously noted are acute myocardial infarction, pulmonary embolism, aortic dissection, pericardial tamponade, and acute mesenteric ischemia.

Case 10: Postoperative Drug-induced Hemorrhage[199]

Patient 1

A 62-year-old male was hospitalized for an elective radical prostatectomy. He had been on no medication other than lisinopril for hypertension, and was not taking over-the-counter drugs or herbal products. The physical examination and laboratory studies were normal. Six hours following surgery he was given 30 mg of ketorolac intravenously for postoperative pain. The following morning he was found to be hypotensive and had one syncopal episode, with a blood pressure of 88/58, a hemoglobin of 6.4 g/dl, and a hematocrit of 16%. The medical staff (prior to obtaining the blood count) considered myocardial infarction and pulmonary embolism as possible diagnoses. Five units of blood were given to maintain a hemoglobin between 7 and 8 g/dl.

Patient 2

A 30-year-old female was admitted for elective hysterectomy, salpingo-oophorectomy, and resection of endometrioses. She was on no medication and was otherwise healthy. A 60-mg intramuscular dose of ketorolac was ordered by the anesthesiologist four and one-half hours postoperatively for pain management. The following morning on attempting to stand, the patient had a syncopal episode. Her blood pressure was 76/44 mm Hg, hemoglobin 6.4 g/dl, and hematocrit 18%. Two units of blood were given to stabilize the hemoglobin at 9 g/dl and a blood pressure of 100/66 mm Hg.

Forensic Implications

Ketorolac is widely used as an emergent non-narcotic analgesic. Poorly realized by the medical profession is the fact that it can seriously affect the coagulation mechanism by its inhibition of platelet function and aggregation. This action is supported in the medical literature. The *Physicians Desk Reference* previously indicated that ketorolac should not be given to patients undergoing gynecologic surgery. Clearly, it should not be given to patients undergoing surgical procedures that are highly vascular in nature, and it should not be utilized with other drugs that can affect the coagulation mechanism. Postoperative recuperation was difficult and complicated for patient 1, who was advised to consider malpractice litigation, which he declined. Undoubtedly, the drug was contraindicated in both cases, which involved an exceptionally high degree of vascularity.

The pediatric medical literature is confirmatory of this conclusion, noting that ketorolac should not be used following tonsillectomy because of serious postoperative bleeding, which has occurred in those cases.

Case 11: Acute Mesenteric Ischemia (Arterial)

A 70-year-old female was admitted with sudden, diffuse abdominal pain. Past and present history was unremarkable except for mild, treated hypertension and hyperlipidemia (cholesterol 232 mg%, triglycerides 185mg%, HDL low at 35 mg% and elevated LDL of 168 mg%). She had no previous symptoms or complaints and was considered to be active, healthy, and young for her given age.

Laboratory studies including the initial complete blood count, sedimentation rate, chemistry profile, amylase, lipase, and cardiac enzymes were normal, as were the ECG and chest x-ray. Ultrasound of the abdomen revealed some sludge in the gallbladder, with a slightly thickened wall. The pain was unrelenting and not alleviated by intravenous narcotic administration, which caused the patient to become comatose and begin to progress to respiratory depression, which was alleviated by intravenous narcan. A CT scan of the abdomen revealed some thickening of the small intestine and ascites, A CT angiogram of the portal and mesenteric system was "unremarkable," and a diagnostic abdominal paracentesis was positive for grossly bloody ascitic fluid.

The white blood cell count several hours later increased to 11,600/μl, and lactic acidosis was present. The pain continued, and the previously firm and distended abdomen became soft and less distended. Thirteen hours after being seen in the emergency room the patient was taken to the operating room, and 7 feet of gangrenous ileum were removed. Fortunately for all concerned, the patient made an uneventful recovery.

Forensic Implications

Acute mesenteric ischemia is one of several medical disaster areas that occur when not diagnosed promptly. The initial and second surgical consultants failed to consider the diagnosis even though the cardiology consultant noted that the patient's course was behaving similar to one of peritonitis. In addition, the fact that all laboratory tests are generally normal at the onset and during the early phase of acute mesenteric ischemia was not appreciated by the initial surgical consultants, placing them in the very precarious position of failure to diagnose and failure to treat. It was estimated that the patient had 4 to 6 hours before the inevitable demise secondary to irreversible acidosis, shock, septicemia, and multiorgan failure would ensue, resulting in malpractice litigation. Had the diagnosis been made within a reasonable 2-hour period, measures to diminish or definitively treat the underlying pathology may have been fruitful.

Mesenteric ischemia remains on the list of the top six diagnoses that are the most frequently unrecognized pathologic entities of which the attending physician must be ever mindful. It is preceded on the list by myocardial infarction, pulmonary embolism, aortic dissection, and pericardial tamponade, in that order, and followed by the sixth diagnosis of equally urgent importance, heparin-induced thrombocytopenia (HIT-2).

Case 12: Subacute and Chronic Mesenteric Ischemia

An 80-year-old female was admitted to the hospital with a burning and squeezing sensation in her throat, of several hours' duration. She was seen in the emergency room three weeks previous for a bout of supraventricular tachycardia, converted to normal sinus rhythm with intravenous adenosine.

The patient's history revealed a diagnosis of primary Raynaud's disease, successfully treated during the winter months, controlled hypertension, and asymptomatic arteriosclerotic cardiovascular disease. Recent gastroenterologic consultation, with upper and lower endoscopy being performed, revealed a diagnosis of gastroesophageal reflux, gastroesophagitis, and diverticulosis with previous diverticulitis.

Initial laboratory parameters included a normal CBC, chemistry profile, and cardiac enzymes. The ECG revealed ischemic type ST-T changes compared to those prior to admission. She was prepared to be taken to the cardiac catheterization laboratory because of the history of new-onset angina with progressive ST-T changes. Shortly before transfer she developed a brief bout of atrial fibrillation, which converted to normal sinus rhythm after the administration of intravenous lanoxin and low-dose beta-blockade. Her fractionated heparin, clopidogrel, and low-dose aspirin were continued.

The following morning it was noted that the patient had paralytic ileus, and the cardiac catheterization was cancelled. A surgery consult was obtained. The patient developed a decrease in blood pressure, increasing sinus tachycardia, and her first abnormal white blood cell count. Hemoglobin and platelet levels were normal. Surgery was cancelled pending further observation in the surgical ICU after transfer from the cardiac ICU. The white blood cell count increased to 23,000, with the hemglobin and platelet counts remaining normal. The abdomen became markedly distended. The patient had no abdominal complaints. Surgery was again scheduled, and then cancelled because of the relatively sudden development of multiorgan failure, preterminal phlebothrombosis, and pulmonary embolism, leading to her demise. Autopsy confirmed the terminal thromboembolic status, 20 to 40% occlusions of diffuse coronary artery disease, the absence of myocardial infarction, and no critical coronary stenotic vascular disease.

The patient's deteriorating status, which led to her chain of "downhill" events and death, was severe chronic occlusive disease of the entire mesenteric arterial system with gangrenous ischemia of the small and large intestines. Severe, diffuse aortic atherosclerosis was also present, but without obstruction or aneurysmal development.

Forensic Implications

In contrast to the previous case, this patient had comorbid and confounding pathophysiologic states, some of which were unrelated, as well as others that were ultimately related to her demise. Those that were highly significant were the diffuse and severe aortic and mesenteric atherosclerosis, which led to thromboembolic disease superimposed upon severe, diffuse mesenteric occlusive thrombosis, causing the most extensive total intestinal gangrene the pathologist had encountered at autopsy. Unfortunately, in this case no therapeutic measures from a medical, invasive, or surgical point of view would have changed the outcome in spite of the initially unexpected diagnosis. Fortunately, however, the family was satisfied by the autopsy report indicating the futility of any medical or surgical measures that may have been considered.

Case 13: Superior Mesenteric Vein Thrombosis

A 60-year-old male was admitted to the hospital as an emergency with the complaints of severe abdominal pain and vomiting of two days' duration. The initial examination revealed generalized abdominal tenderness and diminished bowel sounds, with the abdomen being soft and nondistended. Several hours later the abdomen became distended, with increased pain on palpation and "guarding and rebound." The CT scan revealed dilated loops of small bowel with mucosal thickening and a cystic area near the head of the pancreas compatible with venous thrombosis. The white blood cell count was normal, with a "shift to the left." The serum amylase, lipase, and chemistry profile were normal. Initial diagnoses were pancreatitis, gallbladder disease, appendicitis, or peritonitis. Surgery was performed and revealed extensive gangrenous infarction of the small intestine, which necessitated resection of approximately 4 feet of the small bowel, and an end-to-end anastomosis was performed. Unfortunately, the patient vomited and aspirated during the induction of anesthesia. He died eight days later of bilateral aspiration pneumonia and multiorgan failure. Autopsy revealed diffuse obstruction of the superior mesenteric and pancreatic–duodenal venous systems. The cause of death was due to extensive bilateral pneumonia and pulmonary edema associated with multiorgan failure, adult respiratory distress syndrome (ARDS), and terminal disseminated intravascular coagulation syndrome (DIC) with a platelet count of 47,000/µl.

Forensic Implications

Mesenteric venous ischemia allows the attending physicians more time to make a diagnosis, especially in the subacute and chronic forms. The severe acute forms usually allow 24 to 48 hours to make a diagnosis by proper testing and clinical observation. Some patients present to the physician with vague symptoms of days, weeks, or months, usually nondescript generalized abdominal pain, out of proportion to the clinical findings on examination of the abdomen. If areas of the bowel are infarcted, bloody stools may be present. Recurrent nausea and vomiting commonly occur. Testing is similar to that utilized for acute arterial mesenteric occlusion and include ultrasonography, CT, and MRI scans, which may be more definitive in detecting thrombi in the superior mesenteric vein, as well as the portal vein in patients with cirrhosis and portal hypertension. Arteriography can differentiate arterial from venous obstruction. Immediate anticoagulation with intravenous heparin may be beneficial as long as initial thrombolysis has not been given. If thrombolysis is successful, heparin can be started at an appropriate time interval thereafter, and permanent anticoagulation with warfarin may be needed as long as no contraindications exist.

In this patient, heparin was not begun until 24 hours prior to the patient's demise. Fortunately, the autopsy revealed a good surgical result with no further thrombosis and satisfactory early healing. If clots were detected, failure to anticoagulate postoperatively would have been included in the plaintiff's lawsuit. The admitting and attending physicians were dropped from the lawsuit on that basis. The anesthesiologist was found negligent on the basis of inadequate and improper induction of anesthesia. The plaintiff's expert indicated that rapid-sequence anesthesia induction with cricoid pressure could have prevented retching and vomiting, followed by placement of an endotracheal tube, which would have prevented aspiration.

The lawsuit was settled out of court for a six-figure sum, with a split payment of 75/25 against the anesthesiologist and surgeon, respectively.

Case 14: Pericardial Tamponade

A middle-aged male was admitted from the emergency room to the coronary care unit complaining of shortness of breath and chest pain. Three weeks previously he was discharged from the hospital following a successful mitral valve repair and placement of a mitral annuloplasty ring for severe mitral regurgitation. The presumptive diagnosis was myocardial ischemia and pre-infarctional angina. He had been taking warfarin, a diuretic with potassium replacement, and an ACE inhibitor. Following admission he was begun on an intravenous heparin protocol, a nitroglycerin patch, and 60 mg of intravenous furosemide. Records reviewed by the attending physician and cardiologist revealed a previous discharge hematocrit of 27% and an emergency room hematocrit of 29%. The prothrombin time was 34 seconds (INR 7.88), and the partial thromboplastin time was 80 seconds. Heparin was continued. The admission ECG was stated as showing anterolateral ischemic T-wave changes. During the middle of the night the nurse noted increased dyspnea, a decreasing blood pressure (as low as 75/40 mm Hg), an increased pulse rate, and abnormal neck vein distension. Supportive measures and morphine were ordered. The A.M. prothrombin time was 50 seconds (INR 15), and the partial thromboplastin time was more than 120 seconds. The heparin was discontinued and intravenous vitamin K was administered.

The bedside echocardiogram was performed by the cardiologist who diagnosed right ventricular collapse and pericardial effusion, causing him to suspect pericardial tamponade, 11 hours after admission. A repeat echocardiogram was performed three hours later and was diagnostic of pericardial tamponade. One hour later, the patient sustained a cardiac arrest, from which he was resuscitated, and a surgical consult was obtained. A pericardial drain was inserted two hours later, and 500 cc of blood and clots were removed. The patient died 24 hours following his admission to the hospital.

Forensic Implications

The patient had postoperative hemorrhagic pericarditis, which was not appreciated by his cardiologist until the patient reached the physiologic "point of no return." Anticoagulants were administered injudiciously and erroneously, which unquestionably intensified the hemorrhagic pericarditis, resulting in a state of terminal pericardial tamponade from which the patient was unable to recover.

The plaintiff's attorney and expert witness claimed the following facts:

1. Failure to check the prothrombin and partial thromboplastin times before administering heparin
2. Failure to consider the diagnosis of early (noncompromising) pericardial effusion

3. Failure to consider the diagnoses of pericardial effusion and tamponade in a timely manner
4. Failure to appreciate the severity of and hemodynamic consequences of pericardial tamponade
5. Failure to obtain appropriate surgical consultation regarding the immediate necessity of emergency treatment (drainage)
6. Erroneously not considering the diagnosis of pericardial effusion "because of the absence of severe cardiomegaly"
7. Failure to relate the decreasing hemoglobin and increasing coagulation times, which would have led to an earlier reversal of the anticoagulation status
8. Failure to appropriately assess and relate the electrocardiographic changes to the diagnosis of pericarditis with effusion
9. Failure to appropriately assess the deteriorating hemodynamic consequences as reported by the nurse

The case concluded with a six-figure out–of-court settlement for the plaintiff, as was expected.

Case 15: Toxic Myocarditis from a "Herbal Energy Capsule"

A 56-year-old male professional presented himself for a cardiology consult at the request of his family physician because of a "rapid heart", new onset. The clinical evaluation revealed an irregularly irregular rhythm at a rate of 146 beats/min, characteristic of atrial fibrillation. Other than obesity and hypertension (B.P. 156/104 mm Hg), the examination was unremarkable. The CBC, chemistry profile, T4 and TSH, and lipid profile were unremarkable, as were the cardiac enzymes. The echocardiogram revealed global hypokinesia with an ejection fraction of 48%. An adenosine stress test with a thallium and technetium scan revealed similar abnormalities. He was hospitalized and placed on warfarin and fractionated heparin, digoxin, quinidine, and atenolol. The heart rate decreased to approximately 86/min and converted to normal sinus rhythm in less than 72 hours. The ECG preconversion (Figure 18.5) revealed atrial fibrillation with a controlled ventricular response, low voltage, poor R-wave progression across the precordium intraventricular conduction defect, left axis deviation, and generalized repolarization abnormalities. The postconversion ECG abnormalities were similar except for normal sinus rhythm. Subsequent follow-up revealed the presence of quinidine-induced thrombocytopenia (platelet count of 86,000/μL). The quinidine was discontinued.

Four weeks later the atrial fibrillation recurred, and disopyramide 100 mg four times daily was prescribed. Pharmacologic conversion to normal sinus rhythm was noted five days later. The platelet count subsequently

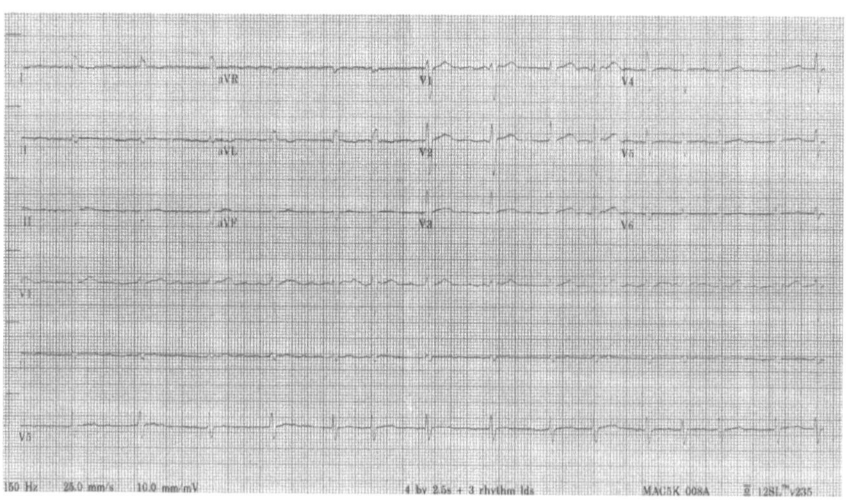

Figure 18.5 Admission ECG. (RuDusky, B.M. Unpublished article. Used with permission.)

normalized. The patient chose not to continue warfarin, and was prescribed 81 mg of enteric-coated aspirin once daily and aggrenox twice daily (time-released dipyridamole 200 mg with 25 mg aspirin, Boehringer Ingelheim Pharma). During the initial consultation the patient noted that he was not taking any medications, however, of his own volition, and on the advice of a friend was consuming an energy supplement. He was advised to discontinue the energy supplement and bring the bottle on his next visit. The capsules contained a multiherbal preparation, which included 24 mg of ephedra.

Forensic Implications

Ephedra is a sympathomimetic stimulating alkaloid, the active constituent being ephedrine. It is known to act as a cardiovascular stimulant causing increased heart rate and hypertension. Other side effects include the production of various cardiac arrhythmias, including ventricular tachycardia, coronary vasospasm, and sudden death. The federal drug administration subsequently legislated that ephedra-containing preparations were to cease being produced and over-the-counter medications containing ephedrine be discontinued. No legal action could be taken against the manufacturers, as the patient was consuming up to nine capsules daily (a total of 216 mg of ephedra), which was markedly in excess of the recommended dose of two capsules daily. After several months his blood pressure became normal and his ECG improved but did not fully recover to normalcy. The patient further noted that he had been taking the preparation for more than two years. He was told by his cardiologist that he was fortunate to be alive and that in all likelihood, he sustained a certain degree of cardiac toxicity that resulted in permanent heart damage (cardiomyopathy). It is important that physicians make an attempt to discover self-prescribed drugs and preparations that patients frequently imbibe, especially when abnormal pathophysiologic states are present.

Case 16: Left Atrial Myxoma

An 81-year-old female complained of having vague, nondescript chest pain. She had a mastectomy for carcinoma at age 51, with no recurrence. There was a possible history of rheumatic fever during childhood. She was receiving appropriate medication for hypertension and hypothyroidism, both of which were well-controlled over the previous 17 years. She gave a history of having two syncopal episodes and one presyncopal episode with no provocation. Physical examination revealed normal vital signs, a grade 2/6 course, short, medium-pitch aortic systolic murmur with slight carotid radiation, and a grade 2/6 high-pitch, blowing, soft, mitral systolic murmur at the apex, with a slight increase in the left lateral position. The ECG was entirely normal, as was the chest x-ray. An echocardiogram revealed slight left ventricular hypertrophy, an enlarged right atrium, mild aortic stenosis, mild mitral regurgitation, stenosis of the aortic and mitral valves, and a 4 × 6–cm left atrial myxoma attached to the atrial septum.

During changes in position, there was no evident ball valve obstruction. The patient refused cardiac catheterization and surgical consultation. In addition to her antihypertension and thyroid medications, she was placed on aspirin and dipyridamole as an anticoagulant regime because of refusal to accept warfarin.

The following year she consulted with a cardiac surgeon who told her not to submit to surgery. She died peacefully at home at age 94.

Forensic Implications

In a situation such as this patient presents, several potential medical–legal points must be considered to avoid malpractice litigation.

1. Failure to diagnose. Appropriate initial diagnostic evaluation was performed. Further evaluation and consultation was advised and refused, the latter being done a year later, at which time the consultant gave his opinion that surgery should not be performed because of age, minimal symptoms, and several comorbid conditions.
2. Failure to appropriately treat. Anticoagulation therapy with warfarin was discussed and recommended, but refused by the patient. At the time, the next-best offering was the combination of aspirin and dipyridamole, which fortunately was successful in preventing the known thromboembolic episodes that may be associated with atrial myxoma.

3. Failure to discuss additional consultation. The patient's refusal of cardiac catheterization was considered to be a denial of a second opinion. Her refusal was based on the fact that she would refuse cardiac surgery.

In this case the second and third consultations and opinions were eliminated by the patient. One year later the family had the patient consult with a cardiac surgeon, who agreed with the patient's opinion, successfully ending the matter. Obviously, and unfortunately, not all similar situations culminate in an outcome as successful and uncomplicated as did this case.

Case 17: Vascular Metastatic Obstruction — Arterial Obstruction Secondary to Metastatic Chondrosarcoma[200]

A 39-year-old male presented to the emergency room because of sudden-onset left hemiplegia and a history of weakness, fatigue, and dyspnea of three weeks' duration. He visited his family physician and was told he had a heart murmur and was prescribed digitalis and a diuretic. The past history revealed that 15 years previously a "lump" was removed from the roof of his mouth, and a bilateral, subtotal maxillectomy was performed. The resulting defect was covered by a dental prosthesis. The lesion was diagnosed as an osteosarcoma. While being examined, he complained of new-onset weakness and numbness of the right leg. Ventricular tachycardia was noted on the monitor and was non-sustained, reverting to sinus tachycardia. In spite of supportive measures consisting of intravenous dextran, fluid replacement, and sympathomimetic agents, his blood pressure continued to decrease. Within 3 hours, the patient expired in refractory pulmonary edema. The postmortem examination revealed 1,000 cc of bloody fluid in the right pleural cavity and clear yellow fluid in the left pleural cavity. The middle lobe of the right lung was adherent to the right atrium, with a 5-cm diameter tumor mass extending into its cavity. The heart and coronary arteries were otherwise unremarkable.

A 7-cm mass was located in the thoracic aorta, and a 5-cm mass was located in the abdominal aorta, completely obstructing the left renal artery and almost completely obstructing the orifice of the right renal artery. Emboli were found in the right common iliac artery, and one was occluding the origin of the left external iliac artery. There were no intimal attachments or attachments of tumor to the endothelial surfaces of any of the blood vessels. The brain was edematous, and a cerebellar pressure cone was noted. An embolus completely occluded the right middle cerebral artery 1 cm from its origin. It contained no tumor cells, the embolus being an embolic blood clot.

Forensic Implications

This was the first case of extensive arterial metastatic chondrosarcoma reported in the world medical literature. Chondrosarcomas are almost totally cartilaginous, with only a minimal amount of supporting connective tissue. Vascular extension is generally by way of the venous system. They have an unusual propensity to grow within the lumen of a vessel without connection to the vessel wall. The arterial source of emboli in this case was the pulmonary vein.

This case is representative of the importance of extracting as much information from past history as possible. It exemplifies the value of an autopsy, often critical in coming to an accurate conclusion of complex and difficult to diagnose situations. The autopsy clearly indicated the futility of any attempt at salvage of life and precludes any attempt at medical–legal confrontation.

Case 18: Oncologic Cardiomyopathy

A 66-year-old male presented to his physician with "a lump in his left neck." Subsequent diagnostic study and biopsy was positive for non-Hodgkin's lymphoma, disseminated to the chest, abdomen, and bone marrow. Physical examination revealed normal vital signs, a split first heart sound, and abnormally palpable lymph nodes in the left neck, left supraclavicular area, and both inguinal areas. The ECG was normal. Initial MUGA (multigated acquisition) scan revealed normal myocardial contractility and an ejection fraction of 59%. The patient was begun on an aggressive chemotherapy program, with MUGA scans taken every two to four months. Initial medication consisted of a combination of thiotepa, velban, and methotrexate. Approximately 13 months later following varying degrees of recurrence, his program was changed to cytoxan, mitoxantrone, adria, and vincristine.

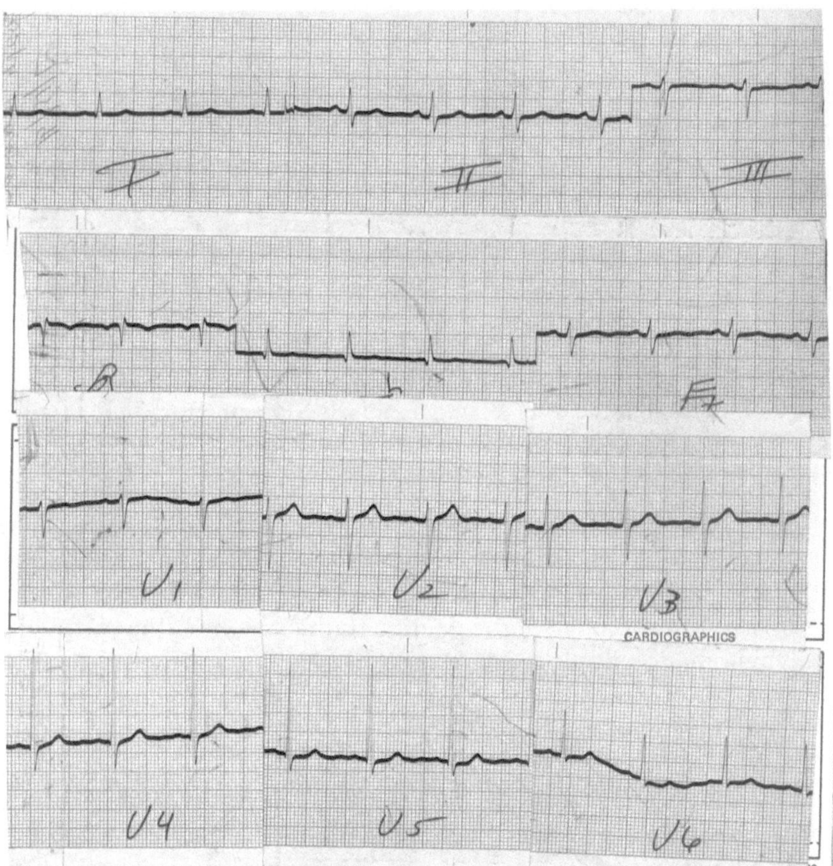

Figure 18.6 Normal ECG pre-chemotherapy. (RuDusky, B.M. Unpublished article. Used with permission.)

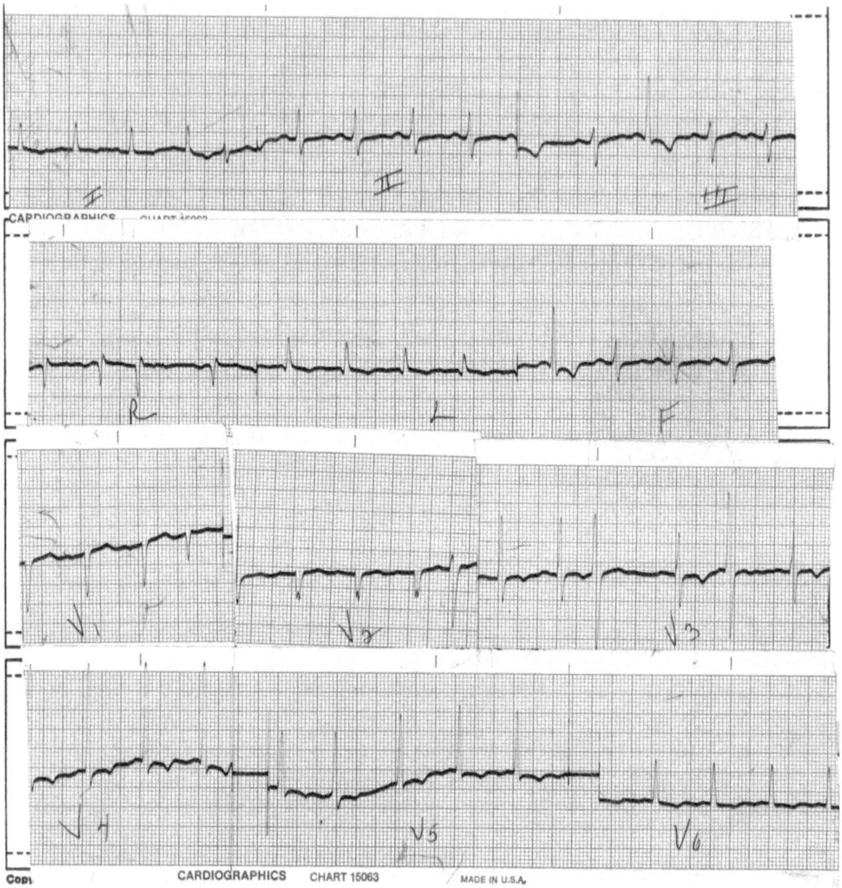

Figure 18.7 ECG after 11 months chemotherapy. NSR, pre-mature atrial and ventricular contractions, generalized repolarization abnormality, "ischemic-type" T-waves and poor R-wave progression in leads V1–V2. (RuDusky, B.M. Unpublished article. Used with permission.)

Careful oncologic and cardiologic follow-up resulted in various alterations of treatment. Over the next 11 months the ejection fractions decreased to 51%, 49%, 29%, and a low of 19%, necessitating continued changes to the program and improvement in the ejection fraction to 49%. The patient developed symptomatic cardiac decompensation noting dyspnea, leg edema, and orthopnea, all of which improved on digoxin, furosemide, and potassium chloride supplementation.

The MUGA scan revealed global hypokinesia, decreased left ventricular contractility, and cardiomegaly. The ECG revealed generalized ST-T abnormality with T-waves of the "ischemic-type." Clinical examination revealed a fourth heart sound (S-4) and a grade 1/6 soft, high-pitched, blowing, nonholosystolic murmur at the apex, compatible with hemodynamically insignificant mitral insufficiency. He continued to improve from an oncologic and cardiac standpoint and survived several years thereafter, his demise being due to recurrent lymphoma. The electrocardiograms before and during chemotherapy are noted in Figures 18.6 and 18.7.

Forensic Implications

As previously reviewed, almost all chemotherapeutic drugs have cardiotoxic potential, some more than others, with a high degree of patient variability. Patients undergoing chemotherapy must be followed closely by the oncologist and internist or cardiologist. As depicted in this case, under diligent observation and study, probably beyond the norm, cardiac complications secondary to chemotherapy occur and must be managed promptly and appropriately to avoid medical–legal involvement. The chemotherapy was withheld following the echocardiographic assessment that showed the ejection fraction (EF) of 29%. In spite of cessation and alteration of therapy, the EF continued to decline (a not unusual situation) and then began to steadily improve on continued variations in the overall treatment program from an oncologic and cardiac point of view. In these cases, dependent upon the clinical assessments and therapies, improvement is not always forthcoming. Myocardial dysfunction can be permanent and may be accompanied by signs and symptoms of congestive heart failure or cardiac decompensation of the non-congestive type.

Case 19: Idiopathic Dilated Cardiomyopathy

A 19-year-old female college student and athlete was seen by a consulting cardiologist with the chief complaints of lightheadedness, weakness, dizziness, and shortness of breath. Her history revealed complaints of nausea, vomiting, headache, and dizziness. Several days later she presented to the emergency room with similar complaints, where a diagnosis of possible vascular headache was entertained. One week later she saw her family physician, and a diagnosis of viral syndrome was made. Three weeks later she was prescribed antibiotics after relating (by phone) that she was not improving. A second trip to the emergency room revealed a positive monospot test, and a diagnosis of mononucleosis was made. Several weeks later, a third emergency room visit was made after she fainted while doing aerobic exercises. A diagnosis of hypoglycemia and anemia was made. Two more phone calls to the family doctor were made with complaints of dyspnea, pounding palpitations of the heart, and chest pain, without being seen by the doctor. Rest was prescribed. During the fifth month of her illness she suffered a cardiac arrest while jogging indoors and was given CPR by a physician in attendance.

She was referred to a cardiologist, at which time her first ECG was done, and a diagnosis of idiopathic dilated cardiomyopathy was made. Several presyncopal episodes occurred sporadically, which led to a complete cardiac investigation. The ECG was abnormal (Figure 18.8), and the echocardiogram

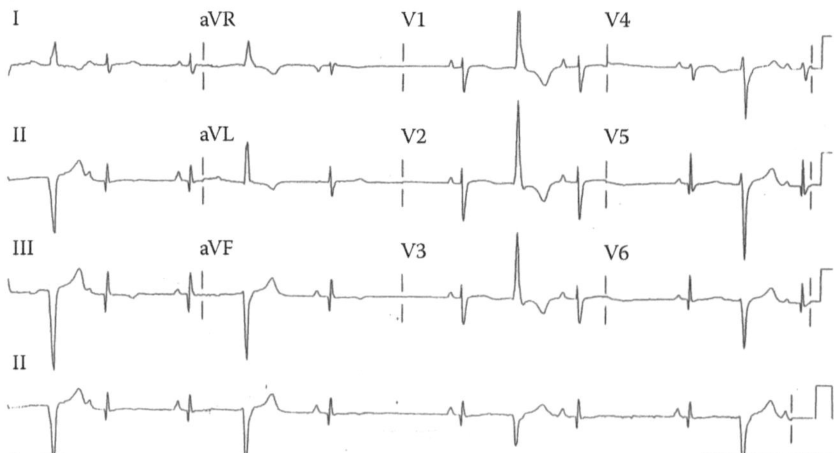

Figure 18.8 ECG revealing sinus bradycardia, ventricular extrasystoles, varying atrioventricular conduction, possible right atrial abnormality, probable infero-lateral fibrosis and generalized myocardial repolarization abnormality and low voltage. (RuDusky, B.M. Unpublished article. Used with permission.)

revealed global hypokinesia and moderate tricuspid and mitral regurgitation with an ejection fraction of 30%. A modified stress test revealed a heart rate of 30 per minute, a blunted blood pressure response, multiple premature ventricular complexes, and nonsustained slow ventricular tachycardia. The scintographic study with thallium revealed "inferior and apical scarring" with a reperfusion response. The signal-averaged ECG was negative for late after potentials. An electrophysiologic study was positive for inducible ventricular tachycardia and ventricular fibrillation. An endomyocardial biopsy revealed myocardial fibrosis, varying degrees of hypertrophy, and chronic inflammatory changes. An internal cardioverter- defibrillator was placed. Over the following two years, progressive cardiac failure ensued. The ejection fraction decreased to 19%. Medical therapy consisted of digoxin, diuretics, potassium replacement, ACE inhibitors, amiodarone, and warfarin. She underwent cardiac transplantation and died two weeks postoperatively of disseminated intravascular coagulopathy and multiorgan failure.

Forensic Implications

Idiopathic dilated cardiomyopathy when progressive (the usual response) has an approximate 50% familial incidence. Most patients are believed to have an inherent genetic chromosomal abnormality with an accompanying immune regulatory dysfunction. It is likely that viral myocarditis is the precipitating factor involved as a "triggering mechanism." The myocardium may exhibit small to large transmural scars in spite of normal epicardial arteries. Intracardiac thrombi are present in over 50% of cases and are an important additional comorbid embolic threat to the entire organ system, as well as to the heart itself, producing nontransmural or elevated ST myocardial infarction. Inherently, disturbances in the coronary microvasculature are known to occur in patients suffering from advanced myocarditis. This produces a decrease in the vasodilator reserve of the coronary microvasculature and can produce subendocardial ischemia in the presence of normal major coronary vasculature.

Legal consultation was sought on the basis of two attending physicians failing to diagnose the recurrent and progressive symptoms that can be associated with cardiac disease. All were attributed to being secondary to mononucleosis in spite of their nonremission and progression.

Additional implications of error included failure to obtain basic studies that should have included, at the very least, a resting ECG, a Holter monitor, repeat laboratory studies, and proper evaluation with follow-up observation and consultation. The plaintiff's experts maintained that earlier diagnosis and therapy would have prevented the near-fatal cardiac arrest and the advanced progression of the disease and allowed the surgery to have taken place at a more opportune time. The conclusion of the attending physicians that this was a case of simple mononucleosis was in error. Myocarditis may occur in cases of mononucleosis, but is considerably more rare than that produced by other viruses. Their assumption that a blood pressure of 74/50 mmHg and the pulse of 48 per minute were both normal in a teen-age female athlete was also in error. A pulse of 48 can be seen in highly trained athletes, but a blood pressure of this low magnitude would be very unlikely. Actuarial tables note that for this age and gender the accepted normal blood pressure varies from a systolic of 100 plus mmHg and a diastolic of 68 to 72 mmHg. The opinion that mononucleosis (Epstein-Barr virus) was the offending agent involved in the precipitation of the myocarditis could not be ascertained, although it was unlikely. The cardiomyopathy probably began after a previous, unrelated viral illness, time of onset indeterminate, the mononucleosis being an additional superimposed burden.

The legal consequences of the case remain unsettled because of the excellence of expert witnesses on both sides rendering the case to one of programmed insolubility. Expert witnesses who are truly such and who possess a high degree of honesty, knowledge, and experience are the most important ingredient in winning a case for the defense or plaintiff. Their assistance in solving the issues may result in a "tie," culminating in a "dropped case."

Case 20: Brugada Syndrome

A middle-aged male presented with a several-year history of presyncope and syncope that had gone undiagnosed until an episode of ventricular tachycardia and ventricular fibrillation was observed during an emergency room visit. He was otherwise healthy, without evidence for underlying medical or cardiac pathology. Eventually, an astute cardiologist recognized the Brugada pattern on the ECG, with the typical "saddle-back" ST-T change in leads V1 and V2. The ECG also showed a probable left atrial conduction abnormality and a nonspecific intraventricular conduction defect (Figure 18.9). A cardioverter-defibrillator was placed and eliminated the syncopal episodes.

The Brugada syndrome is a cardiac oddity believed to be due to a genetic discrepancy involving the myocardial electrolyte action current. It has familial clustering, which requires evaluation and observation for symptoms, with or without associated ECG changes, and must be differentiated from right ventricular dysplasia, which usually features ischemic-type t-wave negativity in the right precordial leads. Both may feature incomplete or complete right bundle branch block ECG patterns. Both the right ventricular bundle block and the "coved" ST elevation has been reported to occasionally be transient in some cases, making the diagnosis quite enigmatic at times.[122] Tada et al. have demonstrated the presence of lipomatous infiltration and fibrosis within the myocardium that is not detectable by the usual endomycardial biopsy and other diagnostic modalities.[201]

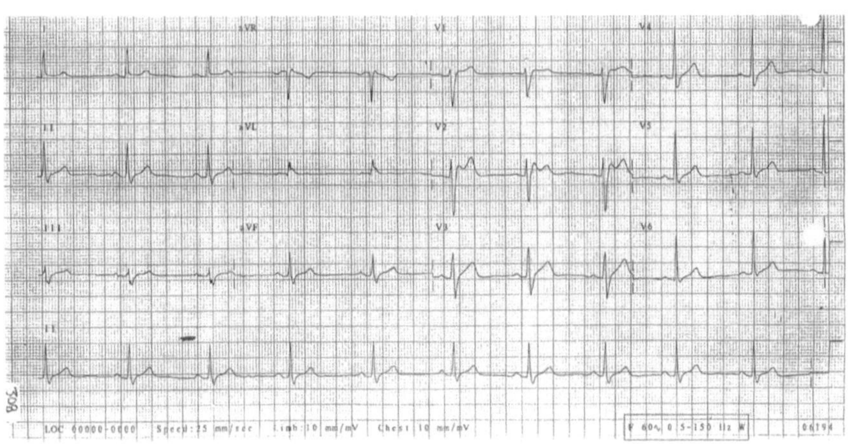

Figure 18.9 The typical depolarization/repolarization pattern is seen in leads V1–V3. (RuDusky, B.M. Unpublished article. Used with permission.)

Forensic Implications

If the patient had succumbed to a cardiac arrest secondary to ventricular tachycardia and fibrillation, it would have taken very little plaintiff testimony to recognize the ECG abnormality and the necessity of preventing sudden cardiac death by an Internal Cardioverter Defibrilletor (ICD). A medical–legal catastrophe was therefore averted.

Case 21: Carcinoid Syndrome[202]

A 39-year-old female with a two-year history of diarrhea and severe weight loss was evaluated in consultation. Numerous laboratory and radiologic studies and upper and lower gastrointestinal endoscopies were negative. Consultation with five gastroenterologists, three at major medical centers, and two hospitalizations were of no diagnostic value and included factitious diarrhea or emotional disorder.

After 19 months the symptoms included flushes and abdominal pain as well as vasospastic angina and bouts of hypotension alternating with hypertension. The patient had undergone a cholecystectomy and hemithyroidectomy. Following her eighth consultation, a urine study for 5-hydroxy indole acetic acid and a serum serotonin level were performed, the former elevated at 46 ng/ml (N = 6), and the latter slightly elevated at 278 ng/ml (N = 260), confirming the suspicion of carcinoid syndrome, most likely affecting the distal ileum. Therapy with several daily subcutaneous injections of octreotide, at great expense, decreased the severity and frequency of the symptoms. Repeat CT scan of the abdomen with radiolabeled octreotide revealed irregularity of the distal ileum.

Forensic Implications

The patient was in a preterminal state of health when seen by her last consultant. She had been contemplating suicide and lost a lucrative professional position. Had the patient remained undiagnosed and untreated and succumbed to her illness, an autopsy would unquestionably have been requested by the family, resulting in law suits against several physicians and institutions and a substantial verdict favoring the plaintiff. The carcinoid syndrome is probably the most overlooked diagnosis causing diarrhea. This is especially true when other associated signs and symptoms of the disease are not evident. Appropriate laboratory and radiographic studies are generally available and of significant value in establishing the diagnosis—as long as it is considered.

Case 22: Stress-Induced Myocardial Infarction

A 48-year-old male was admitted to the hospital for acute chest pain. His history was unremarkable except for a history of hemodynamically insignificant mitral insufficiency and rheumatic fever as a child. The chest pain was precordial in location, with no radiation, and was described as a crushing heaviness. It began within several minutes after hearing an enormous explosion, which shook his home (followed by a fright and flight reaction as he quickly exited from his home). He stated that he thought the area was being bombed.

He was taken by ambulance to the emergency room and was diagnosed as having an acute anterior myocardial infarction, confirmed by ECG and cardiac enzyme determination. Cardiac catheterization revealed mild to moderate mitral regurgitation and no significant coronary arterial obstructive disease, the left anterior descending coronary artery having only a 20% narrowing located in the distal third portion.

Forensic Implications

The explosion was caused by a leaking natural gas line. Initially, the gas company and insurance provider opined that the patient suffered from inherent coronary artery disease, and the heart attack was merely coincidental. Fortunately, the cardiac catheterization was done and supported the fact that the myocardial infarction was stress-related. No further disagreements were made, and the case was settled for a six-figure sum.

Acute cardiac events secondary to a stress-related incident generally occur within minutes to 2 hours after a stressful event, and less frequently up to 12 hours later, depending on the inciting circumstances and whether or not the patient has preexisting coronary artery disease. In this case it was felt that the fright caused by the explosion triggered severe coronary vasospasm leading to acute myocardial ischemia, resulting in a myocardial infarction.

The vast majority of so-called stress-related cardiac events ascribed to physical or emotional circumstances have little or no merit in terms of causation, contrary to the legal and judicial conclusions. Most are due to unrelated circumstances and the not unexpected progression of the patient's inherent disease state. Often, decisions are made that are contrary to independent and neutral expert opinion, including the overt lack of medical and scientific fact.

Case 23: Pulmonary Embolism

A 72-year-old female complained of progressive shortness of breath of one week's duration, intensifying the day she telephoned her physician. She was told not to come to his office but should immediately go to the emergency room, from which she would be admitted to the hospital. She was diagnosed during the telephone conversation as having a pulmonary embolism simply because of the obvious dyspsnea while talking on the phone. Four weeks previously she underwent a laparoscopic herniorrhapy without complications and was discharged the following day. She was obese, and was a well-controlled hypertensive, type 2 diabetic. Her ambulatory ability was diminished because of marked osteoarthritis of the knees. A diagnosis of cardiac syndrome X was made two years previously with complaints of angina pectoris relieved by nitroglycerin. A cardiac catheterization was negative except for minimal coronary arterial plaque formation. It was felt that she had small vessel coronary arterial dysfunction. Her treatment program consisted of long-acting dipyridamole, aspirin, a statin, lisinopril, hydrochlorothiazide, potassium replacement and, metformin. Laboratory investigation revealed a 12-fold elevation of the D-dimer level and normal troponin I and BNP levels. A chest x-ray was unremarkable. Venous ultrasound was positive for a left popliteal vein thrombus. A CT scan revealed extensive pulmonary emboli of both main pulmonary arteries and saddle emboli at their trifurcation. Intravenous heparin and warfarin were started in the emergency room prior to ordering the laboratory tests and scans because of the high clinical suspicion of pulmonary embolism.

Forensic Implications

The history also revealed that the patient was taking arimidex (anastrozole, Astra Zeneca) for one year following a lumpectomy for breast cancer. The drug is known to predispose one to venous thromboembolic events, although infrequently compared to its counterparts. The patient had all of the predominant risk factors known to cause venous thromboembolism: postoperative status, obesity, immobility, and pharmaceutical predisposition. Emergency therapy was promptly administered on the correct assumption of clinical probability and proven by appropriate laboratory investigation. This combination, although not always possible, was unquestionably lifesaving in view of the extensiveness of her disease and severity of symptoms. She was closely observed for the possible need of thrombolytic therapy or surgical intervention, either of which may be necessary in cases of extensive pulmonary thromboembolism. Fortunately, she responded to the accepted therapeutic measures and did not deteriorate, because of appropriate and immediate diagnosis and treatment. Pulmonary embolism is frequently overlooked as a diagnosis, especially when equivocal symptoms and tests are present. It ranks as number 2 in the list of 6 diagnoses for which attending physicians must keep a constant vigil:

1. Acute myocardial infarction
2. Pulmonary embolism
3. Aortic dissection
4. Pericardial tamponade
5. Acute mesenteric ischemia
6. Heparin-induced thrombocytopenia

Pulmonary embolism probably still remains the commonest unrecognized cause of morbidity and mortality, principally because of its frequency, whereas acute mesenteric ischemia is the diagnosis most likely to be completely overlooked. The sixth diagnosis, heparin-induced thrombocytopenia (HIT), completes the list of medical problems that necessitate rapid diagnosis and treatment.

Case 24: Radiation-Induced Cardiac Disease

A 41-year-old male was admitted to the hospital because of anginal chest distress. Cardiac catheterization revealed severe multivessel coronary artery disease with 70 to 90% occlusions of all three main coronary arteries and the first obtuse marginal branch, necessitating a quadruple coronary bypass procedure. Pericardial scarring was present, and additional diagnoses were aortic stenosis and insufficiency, tricuspid insufficiency, and mitral insufficiency. Stenosis in the 70% range was present in the right carotid artery. Valvular and annular calcification was present, which was also noted in the proximal aorta. Fifteen years previously the patient underwent significant radiation therapy to the neck and chest for Hodgkin's lymphoma. He was a nonsmoker and was being treated for hypertension and hypothyroidism, both under good control. Following several complications of his radiation therapy, he developed an effusive pericarditis, eventually leading to surgical treatment with a pericardial window. He applied for disability on the basis of work-related, stress-induced cardiac disease.

Forensic Implications

It was apparent to the independent medical examiner and to the patient's cardiologist that the patient had radiation-induced pericarditis, coronary arterial vasculitis with occlusive disease, and radiation-induced disease of the carotid artery and three heart valves. His application for occupational-induced cardiovascular disease on the claim of "job stress" was denied, and he subsequently was awarded social security disability benefits. Cases of this type exemplify the need for knowledgeable and highly experienced medical experts who possess considerable familiarity with the medical literature.

Case 25: Carbon Monoxide Toxicity

A middle-aged husband and wife presented to their respective family physicians with a multitude of complaints. The wife was a two-pack-per-day cigarette smoker and the husband was a nonsmoker. The wife was previously admitted to the hospital for gynecologic surgery during which a carbon monoxide (CO) blood level of 7.25% was noted (laboratory normal being 0 to 1.5%). This CO level would not be unusual for a cigarette smoker. The varying symptoms of both patients, which "waxed and waned" over a period of one year, included lethargy; depression; irritability; memory deficit; anorexia; headaches; irritation of the throat, eyes, and lungs; and insomnia. Shortly thereafter the husband developed neuro-motor dysfunction characteristic of Parkinson's disease. Of additional interest was the fact that two of three dogs in the household died, and all suffered hair loss, one dog having near total hair loss. Plants in the house also suffered from failure to thrive, which was never known to occur in the past. Investigation by several professional services concluded that the entire household—human, animal, and plant life—suffered from chronic CO poisoning caused by improper installation of a new furnace.

Forensic Implications

CO exposure of varying dose and duration is known to affect neurotransmitter metabolism, resulting in central and peripheral neurologic abnormalities. The patients in this case, as well as the plants and animals, suffered from chronic low-grade CO toxicity over a period of one year. Heavy exposure can cause a mixed sensory–motor neuropathy. Movement disorders of the Parkinson's type are known to occur, in addition to hypotonia, dystonia, and disorders of locomotion. Carboxyhemoglobin levels in smokers can vary from 3% to a high of 18% (normal generally being 0.5 to 1%). In addition to the symptoms suffered by the husband and wife as noted in this case report, generalized weakness, visual impairment, and syncope are known to occur. Dependent upon various factors, mood and behavioral disturbances may present themselves with depression that may be long term. Second-hand cigarette smoke contains twice the amount of CO as the directly inhaled smoke of a cigarette smoker. The half-life of CO is approximately 5 hours. CO damages vulnerable areas of the brain including the globus pallidus and substantia nigra. This can result in tremors and a decrease in motor speed, reaction time, and manual dexterity. Delayed neurotoxicity varies in incidence from 2 to 30%.

Short-term exposure to CO can cause angina and myocardial infarction in patients with coronary artery disease. Continued long-term exposure can accelerate the production or progression of arterial atherosclerosis, all complications being magnified in cigarette smokers and those exposed to second-hand smoke. Delayed neurologic and psychiatric symptoms from 3 to 240 days may occur in 10 to 30% of patients. Recovery from these signs and symptoms may take place in 75% of individuals within one year, but some may remain permanently. The plaintiff's case was settled for a substantial but undisclosed monetary award without necessitating a court trial.

Appendix A: The RuDusky Classification—The World's First Complete Classification of Myocardial Contusion and Blunt Cardiac Trauma

RuDusky, B.M. *Angiology*, 58: 610–613, 2007. Reprinted in modified form with permission, SAGE Publications.

Abstract

Myocardial injury due to blunt chest trauma has been recognized with increased frequency over the past two decades. Increased awareness by physicians and increased use of various clinical and laboratory diagnostic modalities have contributed to this recognition. Injuries range from inconsequential to catastrophic and can affect any or all areas of the heart: pericardium, myocardium, coronary arteries and veins, chordae, papillary muscles, valves, and great vessels. In addition to the medical importance of the diagnosis, many forensic implications have been known to arise. It is important to properly assess and classify the extent of the trauma and its prognostication as to the possibility of residual sequelae. A proposed classification is presented that has both medical and legal applications. The utilization of stages 0 (suspect), I (mild), II (moderate), III (severe), and IV (catastrophic) are illustrated in detail.

Introduction

Trauma remains the leading cause of death in the younger to middle-aged segment of our population.[1,2] Blunt chest trauma causing injury to the heart, frequently due to motor vehicle accidents, has received increased attention in hospital and emergency treatment centers, as well as in the medical literature. Other causes of blunt cardiac injury are numerous, and include falls, accidental and criminal trauma, crush injuries, explosions, and numerous types of sport injuries. Cardiac injury is said to occur in approximately 15% of patients who give a history of blunt chest trauma.[3] Injury to the various structures of the heart occurs as a result of direct kinetic injury by way of high velocity, forceful blows to the chest (baseball, hockey puck, karate kicks, etc.), compression between the sternum and vertebral column, increases in intraventricular volume and pressure as a result of crush-type injuries to the thorax and abdomen, and sudden deceleration that produces injury by a combination of factors related to stretch, torsion, and cessation of propulsion inherent to the kinetic energy or to secondary mechanical trauma (contrecoupe injury to the cardiac chambers). Myocardial contusion is the commonest form of blunt cardiac injury. Its reported incidence varies from 7% to 55 in reported cases of chest trauma.[4] Physicians must be aware that any structure of the heart can be injured in various degrees of severity, either singularly or in any combination, depending on the type and force of the trauma.

No classification is presently available to quantify or qualify the extent of myocardial and cardiac structural injury. Due to the increasing prevalence of medical–legal (forensic) implications regarding cardiac trauma, a classification that has both medical and legal application is presented here.

Discussion

Although the incidence of cardiac injury currently associated with motor vehicle accidents is probably decreasing; its awareness by physicians, as well as various groups of nonmedical personnel, is undoubtedly increasing. The use of active and improved passive restraint systems accounts for the surmised decrease under these circumstances. Pathologically, myocardial injury (muscle) can vary in type and extent from the mildest, consisting of grouped petechiae, to more prominent ecchymoses of the epicardium, which can increase in severity to deeper hemorrhagic lesions (bruising) and in the severest form, myocardial necrosis. The latter can be primary, involving direct muscle trauma, or secondary to coronary arterial injury, occlusion, and subsequent infarction. Larger or more severe primary myocardial lesions may also progress to frank necrosis, which, in turn, can lead to aneurysmal formation, pseudoaneurysms of a cardiac chamber, or direct rupture. Hemorrhage into an intact pericardium can produce sudden or delayed cardiac tamponade, and its resultant fatal physiologic consequences if not diagnosed and treated accordingly.

High-velocity blows to the chest causing sudden death (commotio cordis) is known to occur in various settings, especially direct hits to the chest from baseballs, hockey pucks, and, rarely, football; karate kicks; and fist blows.[5,6] The mechanism causing sudden death in these cases appears to be ventricular fibrillation. Under these circumstances, one cannot assume that myocardial contusion would be absent in all cases simply because its appearance would not have had the opportunity to develop because of the immediate cessation of cardiac activity and life.

The majority of cases of blunt chest trauma are believed to be of minor or negligible importance. As illustrated in Table I, they can be suspected, but will remain unproven and nondiagnosable either because of their nonexistence or their negligible benignity. There will be no historical, medical, or laboratory evidence of their existence, and triage can be successfully completed over a brief period of time and with minimal economic expenditure.

Next in frequency of occurrence are injuries that are classified as mild (stage I) and are also most frequently overlooked, misdiagnosed, or misunderstood (Table II). Symptoms and signs associated with this stage are minor, of brief duration, of minimal significance, and are not associated with major laboratory abnormalities. Although limited follow-up is advised, it need not be prolonged or costly.

In all likelihood, the most problematic area from a medical and legal standpoint revolves around the injury classified as moderate (stage II), as shown in Table III. This category often presents the greatest problems in evaluation, diagnosis, treatment, and follow-up.[7] It is also the category most likely to be misinterpreted by most of the medical profession, often leading to erroneous medical decisions and conclusions. These are known to lead to subsequent legal difficulties, which could generally be avoided if the categorization was properly assessed and fully understood.[8] Significantly greater follow-up from both laboratory and clinical standpoints is advised, although not uniformly

Table I Stage 0 (suspect)

No cardiac symptoms
No cardiac arrhythmias other than mild sinus tachycardia
No ECG abnormalities (normal ECG or unchanged from previous by comparison)
No elevation or slight elevation (borderline) of cardiac enzymes (cardiac troponin I or T)
No echocardiographic abnormality
No scintographic abnormality
Normal chest x-ray
No residual sequelae

Table II Stage I (mild)

Minimal cardiac symptoms of brief duration and limited extent, (angina-like chest pain, atypical chest pain, palpitations)
No arrhythmias other than sinus tachycardia and atrial or ventricular extrasystoles
Minimal, transitory changes of ST segments or T waves on electrocardiogram (repolarization, ischemic, pericardial)
Unequivocal elevation of cardiac enzymes of mild degree
No echocardiographic abnormality
No scintographic abnormality
Normal chest x-ray
No residual or permanent sequelae

Table III Stage II (moderate)

Significant or protracted cardiac chest pain
Marked sinus tachycardia
Frequent premature atrial or ventricular extrasystoles
Supraventricular arrhythmia, either transitory and self-limited or requiring minimal intervention
Significant and more persistent ST-T wave abnormalities of several days' duration or longer (repolarization, ischemic, pericardial)
Moderate, significant elevation of cardiac enzymes
Echocardiographic evidence of mild, temporary hypokinesia or dyskinesia; minimal pericardial effusion, if present
Abnormal scintographic study
Chest x-ray may or may not reveal signs of external trauma (fractured ribs, sternum)
No permanent sequelae

Table IV Stage III (severe)

Severe intermittent or persistent cardiac chest pain
Marked, persistent sinus tachycardia
Supraventricular arrhythmia requiring aggressive therapy
Ventricular arrhythmia
Protracted, significant ST-T wave abnormalities (repolarization, ischemic, pericardial, injury current)
Markedly elevated cardiac enzymes, or moderate elevations of longer duration than expected
Grossly abnormal echocardiographic abnormalities (marked hypokinesia, dyskinesia, akinesia, pericardial effusion)
Easily discernible, grossly abnormal scintographic study
Evidence of acute myocardial infarction resulting from primary muscle injury or secondary to coronary arterial injury (thrombosis, laceration)
Arteriovenous fistula
Pericardial laceration
Valvular disruption not requiring immediate medical or surgical therapy (annulus, leaflet, chordae)
Chest x-ray evidence of external and internal trauma (pleural effusion, pulmonary contusion, possible mild pulmonary vascular congestion)
Possibly permanent or delayed serious sequelae

recommended by those interested in this area of medical practice. In spite of the medical–legal problems that may arise, one can generally be confident that in most instances, no permanent or adverse sequelae will occur.

Patients classified as severe, (stage III), as illustrated in Table IV require immediate expert attention, evaluation, and appropriate therapeutic measures as deemed necessary by the medical team in a well-defined intensive care hospital setting. Long-term definitive follow-up by a medical expert

Table V Stage IV (catastrophic)

Severe systemic signs and symptoms (cardiac, pulmonary, vascular)
Acute, severe valvular dysfunction requiring immediate medical or surgical intervention (papillary muscle, multiple chordae, severe valve disruption)
Herniation of heart through pericardial laceration with signs and symptoms of major vascular obstruction requiring immediate intervention
Pericardial tamponade
Acute, severe congestive heart failure requiring immediate, highly aggressive intervention.
Ventricular or atrial septal rupture
Great vessel laceration
Myocardial aneurysm
Myocardial pseudoaneurysm
Myocardial rupture
Permanent sequelae or death highly probable.

Table VI Basic Classification

Stage	Description	Characteristics
Stage 0	Suspect	No definitive clinical or laboratory parameters
Stage I	Mild	Insignificant clinical diagnosis; no residual sequelae
Stage II	Moderate	Significant clinical diagnosis; no permanent sequelae
Stage III	Severe	Critical clinical diagnosis; may have delayed or permanent sequelae
Stage IV	Catastrophic	Permanent sequelae or death

familiar with such problems is necessary, as serious or permanent sequelae are known to occur. Delayed myocardial rupture, aneurysmal formation, signs and symptoms of progressive or delayed valvular insufficiency, and significant muscle injury with or without coronary arterial injury are likely to be present at some point during the peri-traumatic period or later, which may go undetected for a considerable period of time afterwards if proper attention and assessment are not afforded these cases.[9,10]

Stage IV patients, classified as catastrophic (Table V), are illustrative of self-explanatory acute states, often fatal, or requiring immediate surgical intervention. Death or permanent sequelae are generally the rule rather than the exception. Increased awareness leading to more sophisticated diagnostic and therapeutic measures have made significant strides in saving some of these patients previously considered unlikely to survive.

Conclusion

Blunt chest trauma causing cardiac injury has been given increased attention over the past two decades. This is due to increased awareness on the part of attending physicians, as well as highly improved diagnostic techniques, which have become widely available.

In addition, proliferating medical-legal consequences have prompted additional awareness from all parties concerned. A newly proposed classification is hereby presented (Table VI), as no such classification is presently in existence. We hope it will establish a basic pathway for the diagnosis, acute care, and subsequent observation and follow-up of these patients.

References

1. James, S., Injury mortality. In: *National Summary of Injury Mortality Data*. U.S. Department of Health and Human Services, Washington, DC, 1996.
2. Price, P.R., Mackenzie, E.J. Cost of injury—United States: A report to congress. *JAMA* 262:2803–2804, 1989.
3. Pretre, R., Chileottm, M. Blunt trauma to the heart and great vessels. *N. Engl. J. Med.* 336:626–632, 1997.
4. Sutherland, G.R., Driedgerm A.A., Holliday, R.L., et al. Frequency of myocardial injury after blunt chest trauma as evaluated by radionuclide angiography. *Am. J. Cardiol.* 52:1099–1103, 1983.
5. Maron, B.J., Poliac, L.C., Kaplan, J.A., et al. Blunt impact to the chest leading to sudden death from cardiac arrest during sports activities. *N. Engl. J. Med.* 333:342–347, 1995.
6. RuDusky, B.M. More on myocardial contusion: with additional insight on myocardial concussion. *CHEST* 112:570–572, 1997.
7. RuDusky, B.M. Cardiac contusion: a diagnostic dilemma. *Angiology* 48:929–930, 1997.
8. RuDusky, B.M. Cardiac troponins in the diagnosis of myocardial contusion. *CHEST* 109:1413–1414, 1996.
9. RuDusky, B.M., Cimochowski, G. Traumatic tricuspid insufficiency. A case report. *Angiology* 53:229–233, 2002.
10. RuDusky, B.M. Myocardial contusion culminating in a ruptured pseudoaneurysm of the left ventricle. *Angiology* 54:359–362, 2003.

Appendix B: Potential Short-Term and Long-Term Cardiovascular Risks of Adjuvant Breast Cancer Systemic Therapy

Jones L.W., Haykowdky M.J., Swartz J.J., et al. Early breast cancer therapy and cardiovascular injury, *J. Am. Coll. Cardiol., 50:*1435–1441, 2007. Reprinted with permission, Elsevier Publishers.

Adjuvant Therapy	Short-Term Effects	Long-Term Effects
	Polychemotherapy	
Anthracyclines	Atrial and ventricular arrhythmias Pericarditis / myocarditis Reduced ejection fraction, cardiomyopathy	Progressive decrease in left ventricular function, often leading to overt heart failure
Alkylating Agents		
Cisplatin	Myocardial ischemia/infarction Hypertension Heart failure Arrhythmias Heart block Endocardial fibrosis	
Cyclophosphamide	Pericarditis/myocarditis Heart failure Atrial ectopy Bradycardia	
Microtubule-targeting drugs		
Taxanes	Bradycardia/atrioventricular block Atrial and ventricular arrhythmias Heart failure Myocardial ischemia	

(*Continued*)

Adjuvant Therapy	Short-Term Effects	Long-Term Effects
Antimetabolites		
Fluorouracil	Heart failure Atrial or ventricular ectopy Myocardial ischemia/infarction	
Capecitabine	Heart failure Atrial or ventricular ectopy Myocardial ischemia/infarction	
Methotrexate	Arrhythmias Myocardial ischemia/infarction	
	Radiotherapy	
	Angina Dyspnea Heart failure Diffuse intimal hyperplasia of coronary arteries/left main stenosis Pericardial effusion Sudden death	Coronary artery disease Pericardial constriction Atherosclerosis Mediastinal fibrosis Carotid lesions Thickening of the pericardium Valvular heart disease
	Endocrine therapy	
Tamoxifen	Venous thrombosis	
Aromatase inhibitors	Unknown at this time	
	HER-2-directed therapies	
Trastuzumab	Left ventricular dysfunction Heart disease	
Angiogenesis inhibitors		
Bevacizumab (not yet evaluated in the breast cancer setting) Adjuvant	Hypertension Myocardial infarction Left ventricular dysfunction Venous thrombosis Stroke Heart failure Angina	

Note: The time-course (early vs. late effects) of cardiovascular risk associated with endocrine therapy, human epidermal growth factor (HER)-2–directed therapies, and angiogenesis inhibitors has not been established, given the relatively short period of time that these agents have been used in early breast cancer management.

Appendix C: Recommended Reading

Acosta, Jr., Daniel. *Cardiovascular Toxicology*. Raven Press: New York.

Bloor, Colin, M. *Cardiac Pathology*. J.B. Lippincott Co: Philadelphia, PA.

DiMaio, Dominick J. and Vincent J.M. DiMaio. *Forensic Pathology*. CRC Press: Boca Raton, FL.

DiMaio, Vincent J.M. and Suzanna E. Dana. *Forensic Pathology*. Landes Bioscience: Austin, TX.

Warkentin, Theodore and Andreas Greinacher. *Heparin-Induced Thrombocytopenia*. Informa Healthcare: New York.

References

1. Lloyd-Jones, D.M., Martin, D.O., Larson, M.G., Levy, D. Accuracy of death certificates for coding coronary heart disease as the cause of death. *Ann. Intern. Med.* 129:1020–1026, 1998.
2. Smith-Sehdev, A.E., Hutchins, G.M. Problems with proper completion and accuracy of the cause-of-death statement. *Arch. Intern. Med.* 161:277–284, 2001.
3. Messite, J., Stellman, S.D. Accuracy of death certificate completion: the need for formalized physician training. *JAMA* 275:794–796, 1996.
4. Lakkireddy, D.R., Gowda, M.S., Murray, C., et al. Death certificate completion: how well are physicians trained and are cardiovascular causes overstated? *Am. J. Med.* 117(7):492–498, 2004.
5. Fox, C.S., Evans, J.C., Larson, M.G., et al. A comparison of death certificate out-of-hospital coronary heart disease with physician adjudicated sudden cardiac death. *Am. J. Cardiol.* 95:856–859, 2005.
6. Shojania, K.G., Burton, E.C., McDonald, K.M., et al. Changes in rates of autopsy-detected diagnostic errors over time. *JAMA* 289:2849–2856, 2003.
7. Kassirer, J.P., Cecil, J.S., Inconsistency in evidentiary standards for medical testimony: disorder in the courts. *JAMA* 288:1382–1387, 2002.
8. Pretre, R., Chilcott, M. Blunt trauma to the heart and great vessels. *N. Engl. J. Med.* 336:626–632, 1997.
9. RuDusky, B.M. Cardiac contusion: a diagnostic dilemma. *Angiology* 48:929–930, 1997.
10. Christensen, M.S., Sutton, K.R. Myocardial contusion: new concepts in diagnosis and management. *Am. J. Crit. Care* 2:28–34, 1993.
11. RuDusky, B.M. Cardiac troponins in the diagnosis of myocardial contusion. *CHEST* 108:1413–1415, 1996.
12. Adams, J.E., Davila-Roman, V.G., Bessey, P.Q., et al. Improved detection of cardiac contusion with troponin I. *Am. Heart J.* 131:308–312, 1996.
13. RuDusky, B.M. Cardiac troponins in the diagnosis of myocardial contusion: an emerging controversy. *CHEST* 112:858–860, 1997.
14. Maron, B.J., Pollac, L.C., Kaplan, J.A., et al. Blunt impact to the chest leading to sudden death from cardiac arrest during sports activities. *N. Engl. J. Med.* 333:337–342, 1995.
15. Frame, S.B. Management of the trauma patient. Part 4. Myocardial contusion. *Intern. Med. Specialist* 10:178–181, 1989.
16. RuDusky, B.M. More on myocardial contusion: with additional insight on myocardial concussion. *CHEST* 112:570–572, 1997.
17. Parmley, L.F., Manion, W.C., Mattingley, T.W. Nonpenetrating traumatic injury of the heart. *Circulation* 18:371–396, 1958.
18. RuDusky, B.M. Myocardial contusion culminating in a ruptured pseudoaneurysm of the left ventricle. *Angiology* 54:359–362, 2003.

19. Yaron, W., Berkenstadt, H., Segal, E. Survival after left ventricular rupture following blunt chest injury. *Am. J. Emerg. Med.* 14:186–188, 1996.
20. Durak, D. Cardiac rupture following blunt trauma. *J. Forensic Sci.* 46:170—172, 2001.
21. Pollak, S., Stellway-Carion, C. Delayed cardiac rupture due to blunt chest trauma. *Am. J. Forensic Med. Pathol.* 12:153–156, 1991.
22. Argudi, G., Marchetti, D. Left ventricular aneurysm caused by blunt chest trauma. *Am. J. Forensic Med. Pathol.* 17:194–196, 1996.
23. Liu, S.M., Sako, Y., Alexander CS. Traumatic tricuspid insufficiency. *Am. J. Cardiol.* 26:200–204, 1970.
24. Yasuura, K., Matsuura, A., Maseki, T., et al. Successful repair of tricuspid regurgitation 46 years after causal blunt trauma. *Scand. J. Thorac. Cardiovasc. Surg.* 30:105–108, 1996.
25. Zhu, J., Quyyumi, A.A., Muhlestein, J.B., et al. Lack of association of Helicobacter pylori infection with coronary artery disease and frequency of acute myocardial infarction or death. *Am. J. Cardiol.* 89:155–158, 2002.
26. Catanzaro, J.N., Makaryus, A.N., Catanese, C. Sudden cardiac death associated with an extremely rare coronary anomaly of the left and right coronary arteries arising exclusively from the posterior (noncoronary) sinus of Valsalva. *Clin. Cardiol.* 28:542–544, 2005.
27. Isner, J.M., Donaldson, R.F., Coronary angiographic and morphologic correlation. *Cardiol. Clin.* 2:571–592, 1984.
28. Vavuranakis, M., Bush, C.A., Boudouylas, H. Coronary artery fistulas in adults: incidences, angiographic characteristics, natural history. *Cathet. Cardiovasc. Diagn.* 35:116–120, 1995.
29. Hsue, P.Y., Salinas, C.L., Bolger, A.F., et al. Acute aortic dissection related to crack cocaine. *Circulation* 105:1592–1595, 2002.
30. Eagle, K.A., Isselbacher, E.M., DeSanctis, R.W. Cocaine-related aortic dissection in perspective. *Circulation* 105:1529–1530, 2002.
31. Coady, M.A., Rizzo, J.A., Elefteriades, J.A. Pathologic variants of thoracic aortic dissections. *Cardiol. Clin. North Am.* 17:615–635, 1999.
32. Nienaber, C.A., Spielmann, R.P., vonKodolitsch, Y. Diagnosis of thoracic aortic dissection: magnetic resonance imaging versus transesophageal echocardiography. *Circulation* 85:434–447, 1992.
33. Weber, T., Hogler. S., Aver, J., et al. D-dimer in acute aortic dissection. *CHEST* 123:1375–1378, 2003.
34. Gowda, R.M., Misra, D., Tranbaugh, R.F., et al. Endovascular stent grafting of descending thoracic aortic aneurysms. *CHEST* 124:714–719, 2003.
35. Coselli, J.S., LeMaire, S.A. Left heart bypass reduces paraplegic rates after thoracoabdominal aortic aneurysm repair. *Ann. Thoracic Surg.* 67:1931–1934, 1999.
36. Papadakis, M.C., Leotiadis, E., Manginas, A., et al. Frequency of coronary artery ectasia in patients undergoing surgery for ascending aortic aneurysms. *Am. J. Cardiol.* 94:1433–1435, 2004.
37. Choi, J.B., Choi, H.S., Kim, N.H., et al. Floating thrombus in the proximal aortic arch. *Tex Heart Inst. J.* 31:432–434, 2004.
38. Park, S.W., Hutchinson, S., Mehta, R.H., et al. Association of painless aortic dissection with increased mortality. *Mayo Clin. Proc.* 79:1252–1257, 2004.

39. Tanaka, S., Komori, K., Okadome, K., et al. Detection of active cytomegalovirus infection in inflammatory aortic aneurysms with polymerase chain reaction. *J. Vasc. Surg.* 20:235–243, 1994.
40. Agmon, Y., Khandheria, B.K., Meissner, I., et al. Is aortic dilatation an atherosclerotic-related process? *J. Am. Coll. Cardiol.* 42:1076–1083, 2003.
41. Lederle, F.A., Johnson, G.R., Wilson, S.E., et al. Prevalence and associations of abdominal aortic aneurysm detected through screening. *Ann. Intern. Med.* 126:441–449, 1997.
42. The United Kingdom Small Aneurysm Trial Participants. Long-term outcomes of immediate repair compared with surveillance of small abdominal aortic aneurysms. *New Engl. J. Med.* 346:1445–1452, 2002.
43. Lederle. F.A., Wilson, S.E., Johnson, G.R., et al. Immediate repair compared with surveillance of small abdominal aortic aneurysms. *New Engl. J. Med.* 346: 1437–1444, 2002.
44. Januzzi, J.L., Sabatine, M.S., Eagle, K.A., et al. Iatrogenic aortic dissection. *Am. J. Cardiol.* 89:623–626, 2002.
45. Kao, C.L., Chang, J.P. Aortic graft pseudoaneurysm secondary to fracture of sternal wires. *Tex. Heart Inst. J.* 30:240–242, 2003.
46. Krajcer, Z., Gupta, K., Dougherty, K.G. Mechanical trauma as a cause of late complications after stent graft repair of abdominal aortic aneurysms. *Tex. Heart Inst. J.* 30:186–193, 2003.
47. Reppert, M.K., Charlton, B.L. Aortic injury in blunt chest trauma: a case report. *Guthrie J.* 59:213–215, 1990.
48. Sevitt, S. The mechanisms of traumatic rupture of the thoracic aorta. *Br. J. Surg.* 64:166–173, 1997.
49. Pasic, M., Ewart, R., Engle, M., et al. Aortic rupture and concomitant transection of the left bronchus after blunt chest trauma. *CHEST* 117:1508–1510, 2000.
50. Alimchandani, A., Ananthasubramaniam, K., Smith, D.G. Intramural hematoma of the left main coronary artery: an intravascular ultrasonographic diagnosis of aortic dissection causing acute myocardial infarction. *Cardiovasc. Rev. Rep.* 23:220–222, 2002.
51. Nemec, J., Garratt, K.N., Schaff, H.V., et al. Asymptomatic occlusion of the left main coronary artery by an aortic pseudoaneurysm. *Mayo Clin. Proc.* 75:1205–1208, 2000.
52. Smith, M.D., Cassidy, J.M., Souther, S., et al. Transesophageal echocardiography in the diagnosis of transmatic rupture of the aorta. *N. Engl. J. Med.* 332: 356–362, 1995.
53. Greendyke, R.M. Traumatic rupture of the aorta. *JAMA* 195:119–122, 1966.
54. Duhaylongsod, F.G., Glower, D.D., Wolfe, W.G. Acute traumatic aortic aneurysm: the Duke experience from 1970 to 1990. *J. Vasc. Surg.* 15:331–343, 1992.
55. Kinzel, T., Spontaneous rupture of the thoracic aortic. *J. Am. Geriat. Soc.* 34:395–398, 1986.
56. Townend, J.N., Davies, M.K., Jones, K.L. Fatal rupture of an unsuspected post-traumatic aneurysm of the thoracic aorta during pregnancy. *Br. Heart J.* 66:248–249, 1991.
57. Degenais, F., Bauset, R., Turcotte, R., et al. Delayed treatment of contained blunt traumatic aortic rupture. *Tex. Heart Inst. J.* 30:229–232, 2003.

58. Borioni, R., Garofalo, M., Seddio, F., et al. Posttraumatic infrarenal abdominal aortic pseudoaneurysm. *Tex. Heart Inst. J.* 26:312–314, 1999.
59. Guhathakurta, S., Agarwal, R., Borker, S., et al. Chronic dissection of the left subclavian artery with pseudocoarctation. *Tex. Heart Inst. J.* 30:221–224, 2003.
60. RuDusky, B.M. Spontaneous carotid artery dissection and stroke. *Angiology* 49:669–670, 1998.
61. Chang, A.J., Mylonakis, E., Karanasias, P., et al. Spontaneous bilateral vertebral artery dissection: case report and literature review. *Mayo Clin. Proc.* 74:893–896, 1999.
62. Pruszczyk, P., Szulc, M., Horszczaruk, G., et al. Right ventricular infarction in a patient with acute pulmonary embolism and normal coronary arteries. *Arch. Int. Med.* 163:1110–1111, 2003.
63. Hull, M.C., Morris, C.G., Pepine. C.J., et al. Valvular dysfunction and carotid, subclavian, and coronary artery disease in survivors of Hodgkin's lymphoma treated with radiation therapy. *JAMA* 290:2831–2837, 2003.
64. Heidenreich, P.A., Hancock, S.L., Lee, B.K., et al. Asymptomatic mediastinal radiation. *J. Am. Coll. Cardiol.* 42:743–749, 2003.
65. Byrd, B.F., Mendes, L.A. Cardiac complications of mediastinal radiotherapy. *J. Am. Coll. Cardiol.* 42:750–751, 2003.
66. Cayenne, S., Manzoor, N., Conrad, A., et al. Radiation-induced coronary artery disease. *Cardiovasc. Rev.* July:21–24, 1998.
67. Horimoto, M., Kodama, N., Takamatso, H. Bilateral internal carotid artery disease secondary to cervical radiation. *Angiology* 47:609–613, 1996.
68. Yokoi, K., Hosoi, E., Akaike, M., et al. Takayasu's arteritis associated with antiphospholipid antibodies. *Angiology* 47:315–319, 1996.
69. Setoguchi, M., Fujishima, Y., Abe, I., et al. Aorto-iliac occlusion associated with a lupus anticoagulant. *Angiology* 48:359–364, 1997.
70. Roguin, A., Edelstein, S., Edoute, Y. Superior vena cava syndrome as a primary manifestation of Behcet's disease. *Angiology* 48:365–368, 1997.
71. Price, D.T., Ridker, P.M. Factor V Leiden mutation and the risks for thromboembolic disease: a clinical perspective. *Ann. Intern. Med.* 127:895–903, 1997.
72. Deitcher, S.R., Caiola, E., Juffer, A. Demystifying two common genetic predispositions to venous thrombosis. *Cleveland Clin. J. Med.* 67:825–835, 2000.
73. Martinelli, I., Cattaneo, M., Panzeri, D., et al. Risk factors for deep venous thrombosis of the upper extremities. *Ann. Intern. Med.* 126:707–711, 1997.
74. Onwuznyi, A., Sachdeva, R., Hamirani, K., et al. Multiple aortic thrombi associated with protein C and S deficiency. *Mayo Clin. Proc.* 76:319–322, 2001.
75. Pugliese, D., Nicoletti, G., Andreula, C., et al. Combined protein C deficiency and protein C activated resistance as a cause of caval, peripheral, and cerebral venous thrombosis. *Angiology* 49:399–401, 1998.
76. Glueck, C.J., Wang, P., Fontaine, R.N., et al. Effect of exogenous estrogen on atherothrombotic vascular disease risk related to the presence or absence of the factor V Leiden mutation (resistance to activated protein C). *Am. J. Cardiol.* 84: 549–554, 1999.
77. Marinelli, M., Greene, K. Bilateral thalamic infarction in a patient with factor V Leiden mutation. *Mayo Clin. Proc.* 74:795–797, 1999.
78. Juul, K., Tybjaerg, A., Schnohr, P., et al. Factor V Leiden and the risk for venous thromboembolism in the adult Danish population. *Ann. Intern. Med.* 140:330–339, 2004.

79. Ewenstein, B.M., Handin, R.I. Understanding the antiphospholipid syndromes. *Intern. Med.* 20:38–44, 1999.
80. Ruiz-Irastorga, G., Khamashta, M.A., Hunt, B.J., et al. Bleeding and recurrent thrombosis in definite antiphospholipid syndrome. *Arch. Intern. Med.* 162: 1164–1175, 2002.
81. Hogan, W.J., McBane, R.D., Santrach, P.J., et al. Antiphospholipid syndrome and perioperative hemostatic management of cardiac valvular surgery. *Mayo Clin. Proc.* 75:971–978, 2000.
82. Kerr, J.E., Poe, R., Kramer, Z. Antiphospholipid antibody syndrome presenting as a refractory noninflammatory pulmonary vasculopathy. *CHEST* 112:1707–1710, 1997.
83. Moll, S., Ortel, T.L. Monitoring warfarin therapy in patients with lupus anticoagulant. *Ann. Intern. Med.* 127:177–185, 1997.
84. Wilson, W.A., Crump, J.W. Addressing current issues in antiphospholipid syndrome management. *J. Musculoskel. Med.* 22:9–20, 2005.
85. Tektonidou, M.G., Varson, N., Ktoulas, G., et al. Cognitive defects in patients with antiphospholipid syndrome. *Arch. Intern. Med.* 166:2278–2283, 2006.
86. Kumar, S., Pruthi, R.K., Nichols, W.L., Acquired von Willebrand's disease. Mayo *Clin. Proc.* 77:181–187, 2002.
87. Shah, M.C., Friedenberg, W.R., Mazza, J.J., et al. Conversion of type 2 von Willebrand disease to type 1 von Willebrand disease associated with repair of valvular heart disease. *Guthrie J.* 71:6–9. 2002.
88. Arjomand, H., Aquilina, P., McCormic, D. Acute myocardial infarction in a patient with von Willebrand disease: pathogenetic dilemmas and therapeutic challenges. *J. Invas. Cardiol.* 14:615–618, 2002.
89. Schutt, M., Kluter, H., Wiedeman, G.J. Coexistence of factor V Leiden and primary antiphospholipid syndrome: a patient with recurrent myocardial infarction and thrombocytopenia. *Kardiol* 89:1067–1071, 2000.
90. Warkentin, T.E., Kelton, J.G. A 14-year study of heparin-induced thrombocytopenia. *Am. J. Med.* 101:502–507, 1996.
91. Warkentin, T.E., Hayward, C.P., Boshkov, L.K., et al. Sera from patients with heparin-induced thrombocytopenia generate platelet-derived microparticles with procoagulant activity: an explanation for the thrombotic complications of heparin-induced thrombocytopenia. *Blood* 84:3691–3699, 1994.
92. Hirsh J, Heddlen, Kelton JG. Treatment of heparin-induced thrombocytopenia. *Arch. Intern. Med.* 164:361–369, 2004.
93. Hirsh, J., Heparin-induced thrombocytopenia: strategies for preventing complications. *CME Today* 2:7–12, 2003.
94. Parker, R.I. Heparin-induced thrombocytopenia: essential elements for the clinician. *J. Respir. Dis.* 25:103–112, 2006.
95. Ohman, E.M. Success of identification and treatment of heparin-induced thrombocytopenia. *Cardiosource Rev. J.* June:23–26, 2007.
96. Wallis, D.E., Kelton, J.G., Tapson, V.F. Heparin-induced thrombocytopenia: is it an underdiagnosed condition? *ACCP Symposia Highlights* 17–20, 2005.
97. Rice, L. Heparin-induced thrombocytopenia: myths and misconceptions. *Arch. Intern. Med.* 164:1961–1964, 2004.
98. Bloom, J., Doggen, C., Osanto, S., et al. Malignancies, prothrombotic mutations, and the risk of venous thrombosis. *JAMA* 293:715–722, 2005.

99. Oldenburg, W.A., Lau, L.L., Rodenburg, T.J., et al. Postpartum dissection of the left main coronary artery. *Clin. Cardiol.* 29:175–178, 2006.
100. Baden, E.Y., Adams, B.D. Critical considerations in mesenteric ischemia. *Emerg. Med.* 36:11–17, 2004.
101. Silva, J.A., White, C.J., Collins, T.J., et al. Endovascular therapy for chronic mesenteric ischemia. *J. Am. Coll. Cardiol.* 47:944–950, 2006.
102. Raza, J.A., Miller, M., Dieter, R.S., et al. Diagnosis and non-surgical management of mesenteric ischemia. *Vasc. Dis. Manage.* 3:223–228, 2006.
103. Wong, B., Murphy, J., Chang, J., et al. The risk of pericardiocentesis. *Am. J. Cardiol.* 4:1110–1114, 1979.
104. Alcan, K.E., Zabetakis, P.M., Marino, N.D., et al. Management of acute cardiac tamponade by subxiphoid pericardiotomy. *JAMA* 247:1143–1148, 1982.
105. Kabukcu, M., Demircioglu, F., Yanik, E., et al. Pericardial tamponade and large pericardial effusion. *Tex. Heart Inst. J.* 31:398–403, 2004.
106. Imazio, M., Demichelis, B., Parrini, I., et al. Recurrent pain without objective evidence of disease in patients with previous idiopathic or viral acute pericarditis. *Am. J. Cardiol.* 94:973–975, 2004.
107. Mevrin, P., Weber, M., Renaud, N., et al. Evolution of the post-operative pericardial effusion after day 15: the problem of late tamponade. *CHEST* 125:2182–2187, 2004.
108. Payne, D.D., DeWeese, J.A., Mahoney, E.B., et al. Surgical treatment of traumatic rupture of the normal aortic valve. Ann. Thorac. Surg. 17:223–224, 1974.
109. Bailey, P.L., Peragallo, R., Karawande, S.V., et al. Mitral and tricuspid valve rupture after moderate blunt chest trauma. *Ann. Thorac. Surg.* 69:616–618, 2000.
110. Veeragandham, R.S., Backer, C.L., Mavrovdis, C., et al. Traumatic left ventricular aneurysm and tricuspid insufficiency in a child. *Ann. Thorac. Surg.* 66:247–246, 1998.
111. Bortolotti, U., Scioti, G., Milano, A. Post-traumatic tricuspid valve insufficiency: two cases of delayed clinical manifestation. *Tex. Heart Inst. J.* 24:223–225, 1997.
112. van Son, J.A., Danielson, G.K., Schaff, H.V., et al. Traumatic tricuspid valve insufficiency. *J. Thorac. Cardiovasc. Surg.* 108:893–898, 1994.
113. Sahian, D.M, Labib, S.B, Chang, G. Cardiac papillary fibroelastoma. *Ann. Thorac. Surg.* 59:538–546, 1995.
114. Davoli, G., Bizzari, F., Tucci, E., et al. Double papillary fibroelastoma of the aortic valve. *Tex. Heart Inst. J.* 31:448–449, 2004.
115. Schoondyke, J.W., Burress, J.W., Shabaneh, B., et al. Papillary fibroelastoma involving the left ventricular wall. *Rev. Cardiovasc. Med.* 4:184–187, 2003.
116. Shing, M., Rubenson, D.S. Embolic stroke and papillary fibroelastoma. *Clin. Cardiol.* 24:346–347, 2001.
117. Edwards, F.H., Hale, D., Cohen, A., et al. Primary cardiac valve tumors. *Ann. Thorac. Surg.* 52:1127–1131, 1991.
118. RuDusky, B.M., Martine, D. *The Carcinoid Syndrome: A Medical, Social and Political Odyssey.* Bookman, Martinsville, IN, 2004:1–4.
119. Schoen, S.P., Kittner, T., Meinhardt, M., et al. Metastatic infiltration of the myocardium presenting with angina pectoris. *Clin. Cardiol.* 29:323, 2006.
120. Brugada, P., Brugada, J. Right bundle branch block, persistent ST segment elevation and sudden cardiac death: a distinct clinical and electrocardiographic syndrome. *J. Am. Coll. Cardiol.* 20:1391–1396, 1992.

121. RuDusky, B.M. Right bundle branch block with persistent ST elevation and ventricular tachycardia. *Angiology* 49:71–72, 1998.
122. RuDusky, B.M. Right bundle branch block, persistent ST-segment elevation, and sudden death. *Am. J. Cardiol.* 82:407–408, 1998.
123. Box, L.C., Hanak, V., Arciniegas, J.G. Dual coronary emboli in peripartum cardiomyopathy. *Tex. Heart Inst. J.* 31:442–444, 2004.
124. Hegde, N., Rich, M.W., Gayomali, C. The cardiomyopathy of iron deficiency. *Tex. Heart Inst. J.* 33:340–344, 2006.
125. Yaliniz, H., Tokcan, A., Salih, O., et al. Surgical treatment of cardiac hydatid disease. Tex. Heart Inst. J. 33:340–344, 2006.
126. Fazio, S., Palmieri, E.A., Ferravante, B., et al. Doxorubicin-induced cardiomyopathy treated with carvedilol. *Clin. Cardiol.* 21:777–779, 1998.
127. Kalay, N., Basar, E., Ozdogru, I., et al. Protective effects of carvedilol against anthracycline-induced cardiomyopathy. *J. Am. Coll. Cardiol.* 48:2258–2262, 2006.
128. Cardinale, D., Colombo, A., Sandri, M.T., et al. Prevention of high dose chemotherapy-induced cardiotoxicity in high-risk patients by angiotensin- converting enzyme inhibition. *Circulation* 114: 2472–2481, 2006.
129. Woods, T., Vidarsson, B., Mosher, D., et al. Transient effusive-constrictive pericarditis due to chemotherapy. *Clin. Cardiol.* 22:316–318, 1999.
130. Rich, M.W. Myocardial injury caused by an anaphylactic reaction to ampicillin/sulbactam. *Tex. Heart Inst. J.* 25:194–197, 1998.
131. Misra, P., Caldito, G.C., Kakkar, A.K., et al. Outcomes of coronary artery bypass grafting in patients with a history of illicit drug use. Am. J. Cardiol. 92:593–595, 2003.
132. Khung-Keong, Y., Wijetunga, M., Ito, H., et al. The association of methamphetamine use and cardiomyopathy in young patients. *Am. J. Med.* 120:165–171, 2007.
133. Conraads, V.M., Jorens, P.G., Ebo, D.G., et al. Coronary artery spasm complicating anaphylaxis secondary to skin disinfectant. *CHEST* 113:1417–1419, 1998.
134. Dhar, R., Stout, C.W., Link, M.S., et al. Cardiovascular toxicities of performance-enhancing substances in sports. *Mayo Clin. Proc.* 80:1307–1315, 2005.
135. Henry, C.R., Satran, D., Lindgren, B., et al. Myocardial injury and long-term mortality following moderate to severe carbon monoxide poisoning. *JAMA* 295: 398–402, 2006.
136. Stern, F.B., Halperin, W.E., Hornung, R.W., et al. Heart disease mortality among bridge and tunnel officers exposed to carbon monoxide. *Am. J. Epidemiol.* 128:1276–1288, 1988.
137. Guidotti, T.L. Occupational mortality among firefighters: addressing the association. *J. Occup. Environ. Med.* 37:1348–1356, 1995.
138. Glueck, C.J., Kelley, W., Wang, P., et al. Risk factors for coronary heart disease among firefighters in Cincinnati. *Am. J. Indust. Med.* 30:331–340, 1996.
139. Kalay, N., Ozdugru, I., Cetinkaya, Y., et al. Cardiovascular effects of carbon monoxide poisoning. *Am. J. Cardiol.* 99:322–324, 2007.
140. Alexander, G.J., Kanner, R.E. Clinical effects of air pollution. *Contemp. Intern. Med.* 8: 9–14, 1996.
141. Suwa, T., Hogg, J.C., Quinlan, K.B., et al. Particulate air pollution induces progression of atherosclerosis. *J. Am. Coll. Cardiol.* 39:935–945, 2002.
142. Brook, R.D., Franklin, B., Cascio, W., et al. Air pollution and cardiovascular disease. *Circulation* 109:2655–2671, 2004.
143. Suwa, T., Hogg, J.G., Quinlan, K.B., et al. Particulate air pollution induces progression of atherosclerosis. *J. Am. Coll. Cardiol.* 39:935–342, 2002.

144. RuDusky, B.M. *Your Car Can Be Hazardous to Your Health.* Authorhouse, Bloomington IN, 2002.
145. Cayenne, S., Manzoor, N., Conrad, Q., et al. Radiation-induced coronary artery disease. *Cardiovasc. Rev. Res.* July:21–33, 1998.
146. Hull, M.C., Morris, C.C., Pepine, C.J., et al. Valvular dysfunction and carotid, subclavian, and coronary artery disease in survivor's of Hodgkin lymphoma treated with radiation therapy. *JAMA* 290:2831–2837, 2003.
147. Heidenreich, P.A., Hancock, S.L., Lee, B.K., et al. Asymptomatic cardiac disease following mediastinal irradiation. *J. Am. Coll. Cardiol.* 42:743–749, 2003.
148. Whittaker, L.A., Kenny, C.C., Grover, F.L., et al. Right-sided heart failure and severe tricuspid regurgitation after mediastinal radiation. *Cardiovasc. Rev. Rep.* 22:23–25, 2001.
149. Pritchett, A.M., Morrison, J.F., Edwards, W.D., et al. Valvular heart disease in patients taking pergolide. *Mayo Clin. Proc.* 77:1280–1286, 2002.
150. Kancherla, M.K., Salti, H.I., Mulderink, T.A., et al. Echocardiographic prevalence of mitral and/or aortic regurgitation in patients exposed to either fenfluramine–phentermine combination or to dexfenfluramine. *Am. J. Cardiol.* 84:1335–1338, 1999.
151. Gardin, J.M., Schumacher, D., Constantine, G., et al. Valvular abnormalities and cardiovascular status following exposure to dexfenfluramine or phentermine/fenfluramine. *JAMA* 283:1703–1709, 2000.
152. Lepor, N.E., Gross, S.B., Daley, W.L., et al. Dose and duration of fenfluramine-phentermine therapy impacts the risk of significant valvular heart disease. *Am. J. Cardiol.* 86: 107–110, 2000.
153. Shively, B.K., Roldan, C.A., Gill, E.A., et al. Prevalence and determinants of valvulopathy in patients treated with dexfenfluramine. *Circulation* 100:2151–2167, 1999.
154. Hensrud, D.D., Connolly, H.M., Grogan, M., et al. Echocardiographic improvement over time after cessation of use of fenfluramine and phentermine. *Mayo Clin. Proc.* 74:1181–1197. 1999.
155. Mast, S.T., Jollis, J.G., Ryan, T., et al. The progression of fenfluramine-associated valvular heart disease assessed by echocardiography. *Ann. Intern. Med.* 134: 261–266, 2001.
156. Weissman, N.J., Panza, J.A., Tighe, J.F., et al. Natural history of valvular regurgitation 1 year after discontinuation of dexfenfluramine therapy. *Ann. Intern. Med.* 134:267–273, 2001.
157. Varriale, P., Fluoxetine (prozac) as a cause of QT prolongation. *Arch. Intern. Med.* 161:617, 2001.
158. Zareba, W., Moss, A.J., Rosero, S.Z., et al. Electrocardiographic findings in patients with diphenhydramine overdose. *Am. J. Cardiol.* 80:1168–1173, 1997.
159. Gabel, A., Schymik, G., Mehmel, H.C. Ventricular fibrillation due to long QT syndrome probably caused by clindamycin. *Am. J. Cardiol.* 83:813–815, 1999.
160. Mishra, A., Friedman, H.S., Sinha, A.K. The effects of erythromycin on the electrocardiogram. *CHEST* 115:983–986, 1999.
161. Orban, Z., MacDonald, L.L., Peters, M.A., et al. Erythromycin-induced cardic toxicity. *Am. J. Cardiol.* 75:859–861, 1995.
162. Katapadi, K., Kostandy, G., Katapadi, M., et al. A review of erythromycin-induced malignant tachyarrhythmia–torsade de pointes. *Angiology* 48:821–826, 1997.
163. RuDusky, B.M. The fifth dimension of electrocardiography. *Vasc. Dis.* 4:26–43, 1967.

164. RuDusky, B.M. Errors of computer electrocardiography. *Angiology* 48:1045–1050, 1997.
165. Bauerlein, T.G., Stobbe, L.H. Acute pancreatitis simulating myocardial infarction with characteristic electrocardiographic changes. *Gastroenterology* 27:861, 1951.
166. Willard, J.H. Cardiac symptoms secondary to gastrointestinal tract disturbances. *Am. Pract. Digest. Treat.* 1:376, 1950.
167. RuDusky, B.M. Electrocardiographic changes associated with neurologic events. *CHEST* 108:884–885, 1995.
168. Samuels, M. Electrocardiographic manifestations of neurologic disease. *Semin. Neurol.* 4:453–458, 1984.
169. Tennant, C., Langeluddecke, P., Fulcher, G., et al. Acute and chronic life event stress in coronary atherosclerosis. *J. Psychosom. Res.* 32:13–20, 1988.
170. Jones, D.R., Heart disease mortality following widowhood: some results from the OPCS longitudinal study. *J. Psychosom. Res.* 31:325–333, 1987.
171. Trevisan, M., Jossa, F., Farinaro, E., et al. Earthquake and coronary heart disease risk factors: a longitudinal study. *Am. J. Epidemiol.* 135:632–670, 1992.
172. Mittleman, M.A., Maclure, M., Sherwood, J.B., et al. Triggering of acute myocardial infarction onset by episodes of anger. *Circulation* 92:1720–1725, 1995.
173. Hlatky, M.A., Lam, L.C., Lee, K.L., et al. Job strain and the prevalence and outcome of coronary artery disease. *Circulation* 92:327–333, 1995.
174. Reed, D., Yano, K. Prediction of arteriographically defined coronary stenosis in the Honolulu Heart Program. *Am. J. Epidemiol.* 134:111–122, 1991.
175. Wellenius, G.A., Schwartz, J., Mittleman, M.A. Particulate air pollution and hospital admissions for congestive heart failure in seven United States cities. *Am. J. Cardiol.* 97:404–408, 2006.
176. Mittleman, M.A. Triggers of acute cardiac events: new insights. *Am. J. Med. Sports* 4:99–102, 2002.
177. Kop, W.J. Chronic and acute psychological risk factors for clinical manifestations of coronary artery disease. *Psychosom. Med.* 61:476–487, 1999.
178. Welin, L., Svardsudd, K., Wilhelmsel, L., et al. Analysis of risk factors for stroke in a cohort of men born in 1913. *N. Engl. J. Med.* 317:521–526, 1987.
179. Purcell, H., Mulcahy, D. Acute myocardial infarction triggered by emotional stress. *Am. J. Cardiol.* 71:494–495, 1993.
180. Macleod, J., Smith, G.D., Heslop, P., et al. Psychologic stress and cardiovascular disease: empirical demonstration of bias in a prospective observational study of Scottish men. *Br. Med. J.* (international ed.) 324:1–7, 2002.
181. Malek, A.M., Alper, S.L., Izumo, S. Hemodynamic shear stress and its role in atherogenesis. *JAMA* 282:2035–2041, 1999.
182. Niebauer, J., Cooke, J.P. Cardiovascular effects of exercise: role of endothelial shear stress. *J. Am. Coll. Cardiol.* 28:1652–1660, 1996.
183. RuDusky, B.M. Mechanical factors in the production of atheromatous disease with a critique on antilipid therapy. *Cardiovasc. Eng.* 3:39–42, 2003.
184. Mittleman, M.A., Maclure, M., Tofler, G.H., et al. Triggering of acute myocardial infarction by heavy physical exertion. *N. Engl. J. Med.* 329:1677–1683, 1993.
185. Willlich, S.N., Lewis, M., Lowel, H., et al. Physical exertion as a trigger of acute myocardial infarction. *N. Engl. J. Med.* 329:1684–1690, 1993.
186. Muller, J.E., Tofler, O.H., Stone, P.H. Circadian variation and triggers of onset of acute cardiovascular disease. *Circulation* 79:733–743, 1989.

187. Franklin, B.A., George, P., Henry, R., et al. Acute myocardial infarction after manual or automated snow removal. *Am. J. Cardiol.* 878:1282–1283, 2001.
188. Albert, C.M., Mittleman, M.A., Chae, C.U., et al. Triggering of sudden death from cardiac causes by physical exertion. *N. Engl. J. Med.* 343:1355–1361, 2000.
189. Kohl, H.W., Powell, K.E., Gordon, N.F., et al. Physical activity, physical fitness, and sudden cardiac death. *Epidemiol. Rev.* 14:37–58, 1992.
190. Siscouick, D.S., Weiss, N.S., Fletcher, R.H., et al. The incidence of primary cardiac arrest during vigorous exercise. *N. Engl. J. Med.* 311:874–877, 1984.
191. Kannel, W.B., Thomas, H.E. Sudden coronary death: the Framingham Study. *Ann. NY Acad. Sci.* 382:3–21, 1982.
192. Giri, S., Thompson, P.D., Kiernan, F.J., et al. Clinical and angiographic characteristics of exertion-related acute myocardial infarction. *JAMA* 282:1731–1736, 1999.
193. Burke, A.P., Farb, A., Malcom, G.T., et al. Plaque rupture and sudden death related to exertion in men with coronary artery disease. *JAMA* 281:921–926, 1999.
194. RuDusky, B.M., Cimochowski, G. Traumatic tricuspid insufficiency. A case report. *Angiology* 53:229–233, 2002.
195. RuDusky, B.M. Myocardial infarction in the very young. *CHEST* 122:1099, 2002.
196. RuDusky, B.M. Acute myocardial infarction in a 16-year-old male. *Angiology* 54: 103–107, 2003.
197. Przybojewski, J.Z., Heyns, M.H. Acute myocardial infarction due to coronary vasospasm secondary to industrial nitroglycerin withdrawal. *S. Afr. Med. J.* 64:101–104, 1983.
198. RuDusky, B.M. Acute myocardial infarction secondary to coronary vasospasm during withdrawal from industrial nitroglycerin exposure. *Angiology* 52:143–144, 2001.
199. RuDusky, B.M. Severe postoperative hemorrhage attributed to single-dose parenteral ketorolac-induced coagulopathy. *Angiology* 51:999–1002, 2000.
200. RuDusky, B.M. Chondroscarcoma: report of a case with extensive arterial occlusion. *Vasc. Dis.* 2:352–356, 1965.
201. Tada. H., Aihara, N., Ohe, T., et al. Arrhythmogenic right ventricular cardiomyopathy underlies syndrome of right bundle branch block, ST-segment elevation and sudden death. *Am. J. Cardiol.* 81:519–522, 1998.
202. RuDusky, B.M., Martine, D. *The Carcinoid Syndrome: A Medical, Social and Political Odyssey.* Airleaf Publishers, Martinsville, IN, 2004.

Bibliography

Akkersdijk, G.J., Puylaert, J.B., deVries, A.C. Abdominal aortic aneurysm as an incidental finding in abdominal ultrasonography. *Br. J. Surg.* 78:1261–1263, 1991.

Aziz, F., Baciewicz, F. Lambl's excrescences: review and recommendations. *Tex. Heart Inst. J.* 34:366–368, 2007.

Bardakci, H., Kervan, U., Boysan, E., et al. Aortic arch aneurysm, pseudocoarctation, and coronary artery disease in a patient with Behcet's syndrome. *Tex. Heart Inst. J.* 34:363–365, 2007.

Bengtsson, H., Bergquist, D., Sternby, N.H. Increasing prevalence of abdominal aortic aneurysms. A necropsy study. *Eur. J. Surg.* 158:19–23, 1992.

Cardinale, D., Colombo, A., Sandri, M.T., et al. Prevention of high-dose chemotherapy-induced cardiotoxicity in high-risk patients by angiotensin: converting enzyme inhibition. *Circulation* 114:2474–2481, 2006.

Cogert, G., Siegel, R.J. Giant floating aortic thrombus: a rare finding on transesophageal echocardiography. *Am. J. Cardiol.* 99:739–740, 2007.

Davies, R.R., Goldstein, L.J., Coady, M.A., et al. Yearly rupture or dissection rates for thoracic aortic aneurysms: simple prediction based on size. *Ann. Thorac. Surg.* 73:17–28, 2002.

Fanoe, S., Hvidt, C., Ege, P., et al. Syncope and QT prolongation among patients treated with methadone for heroin dependence in the city of Copenhagen. *HEART* 39:1051–1055, 2007.

Feenstra, J., Grobbee, D.E., Remme, W.J., et al. Drug-induced heart failure. *J. Am. Coll. Cardiol.* 33: 1152–1162, 1999.

Gaita, F., Giustetto, C., Bianchi, F., et al. Short QT syndrome: a familial cause of sudden death. *Circulation* 108:965–970, 2003.

Goel, S., Clair, D.G., Carman, T.L. An 18-year-old with effort-related arm swelling. *Cleveland Clin. J. Med.* 74:283–288, 2007.

Griep, R.B., Ergin, A., Galla, J.D., et al. Natural history of descending thoracic and thoraco-abdominal aneruysms. *Ann. Thorac. Surg.* 67:1927–1930, 1999.

Guimaraes-Filho, F., Doralice, T., Braga, J., et al. Ventricular systolic reserve in asymptomatic children previously treated with low doses of anthracyclines. *Am. J. Cardiol.* 100:1303–1306, 2007.

Harris, E.E., Correa, C., Hwang, W.T., et al. Late cardiac mortality and morbidity in early-stage breast cancer patients after breast-conservation treatment. *J. Clin Oncol* 24: 4100–4106, 2006.

Kopf, G.S., Rizzo, J.A., Management of descending aortic dissection. *Ann. Thorac. Surg.* 67:2002–2005, 1999.

Mehta, R.H., Manfredini, R., Hassan, F., et al. Chronobiological patterns of acute aortic dissection. *Circulation* 106:1110–1115, 2002.

Mehta, R.H., O'Gara, P.T., Bossone, E., et al. Acute type A aortic dissection in the elderly. *J. Am. Coll. Cardiol.* 40:685–692, 2002.

Rogers, I.S., Rinaldi, M.J., Humphrey, C.B., et al. Postpartum dissection of the left main coronary artery. *Clin. Cardiol.* 29:175–178, 2006.

Scally, N., O'Donnell, M.E., McClintock, C., et al. Mesenteric artery occlusion secondary to activated protein C resistance. *Angiology* 58:768–771, 2008.

Schimpf, R., Wolpert, C., Gaito, F., et al. Short QT syndrome. *Cardiovasc. Res.* 67: 357–366, 2005.

Sehdey, A.E., Hutchins, G.M. Problems with proper completion and accuracy of the cause of death statement. *Arch. Intern. Med.* 161:277–284, 2001.

Stajdur, K.C., Laired, J.R., Rogan, K.M., et al. Coronary artery ectasia: increased prevalence in patients with abdominal aortic aneurysm as compared to occlusive atherosclerotic peripheral vascular disease. *Am. Heart J.* 125:86–92, 1993.

Warkentin, T.E. Heparin-induced thrombocytopenia. Part 1. The diagnostic clues. *J. Crit. Illness* 201:6–13. 2005.

Index

D

Q

R